The Bench

by

Jeff Brown

much love – Jeff x 23.09.23

All rights are strictly reserved and application for performance or other uses should be made before rehearsal to Southbank Communications, Kelvey House, Jarrow, Tyne & Wear NE32 5BH.

T: 07949 765 426.   E: Jeffbrowntv@gmail.com.

All characters appearing in this work are fictitious. This play contains material of a sensitive nature and is recommended for age 15+.

ISBN: 978-1-7397169-0-5

First published by KELVEY September 2023

Printed and Bound by Martins the Printers Ltd of Berwick upon Tweed.

Author's note

Two plays – one fact, one fiction - both delving into the underside of football. *Cornered* is the true story of one man's treatment at the hands of fans who could not forgive a simple mistake. *The Bench*, set more than thirty years later, highlights the challenges footballers face today.

Acknowledgements

For *The Bench*, I'd like to thank Ray Spencer at The Customs House, director Olivia Millar-Ross, producer Natasha Haws and all the original cast, along with those who have encouraged and supported me in the development of *The Bench*: Paul and Nessa Dunn, for inviting me to submit the outline of the play to a scratch night at The Peacock pub in Sunderland in 2018; Ed Waugh, Melanie Hill and Jimmy Daly for their encouragement in developing the work; my daughter, Alice Stokoe for her professional guidance and – above all – my wife, Susan Wear, for her patience, unwavering support and forensic attention to detail.

Jeff Brown

September 2023

Original cast

The Bench was first performed at The Customs House in South Shields 20-23 September, 2023. It was directed by Olivia Millar-Ross. The brilliant cast and creative team were:

Adi Dokobu	Jason Njoroge
Vicky Sanderson	Hannah Marie Davis
Mike Mulligan	Adam Donaldson
Ange/Steward	Abigail Lawson
Lad/Darren	Dan Howe
Boy	Zac Anders
Radio commentator	Nick Barnes
Radio presenter	Gilly Hope
Producer	Natasha Haws
Production Designer	Lee Ward
Lighting Designer	John Rainsforth

Synopsis

It's August 2017, in a northern town where happiness appears to hinge around the fortunes of the local football team and the transfer window is closing. With austerity biting and social care becoming a heavy burden the state seems unwilling to bear, single mum Vicky is finding life a struggle.

Her own mother is ill, her baby's father isn't around, so the daily trip to the local park has become a welcome – if brief – escape from reality.

Adi has had struggles of his own, leaving the Congo as a child to escape the Great African War. Raised in France by adoptive parents, he finds an outlet for his frustrations through football. Success brings him financial rewards, and a big-money move to the English Premier League – but can it buy him happiness?

And when their two – seemingly disparate - worlds collide, by a chance meeting on a park bench, can they find common ground which might keep them together?

Characters

ADI DOKOBU - Aged early 20s, a black footballer who left the Congo as a boy to escape the Great War of Africa and was raised by his adoptive parents in the French city of Montpellier. He speaks good English, with a French accent.

VICKY SANDERSON - Aged early 20s, a single mum whose determination keeps her family together.

MIKE MULLIGAN - Aged early 30s, a football agent who works for Adi. He has a Scouse accent.

ANGE - Aged early 20s, Vicky's best friend.

LAD/DARREN - Aged 17/18, lad in park, footballer

BOY - Aged about 10

RADIO COMMENTATOR - Can be pre-recorded

RADIO PRESENTER – Can be pre-recorded

STEWARD

Act 1

Scene 1

August, 2017. Wednesday afternoon. A local park. Vicky has her baby son, Georgey, in his buggy. They stop at a bench, overlooking the bowling green. She is singing to the baby when Adi walks by. He stops suddenly when he recognises the song.

VICKY: Frere Jacques, Frere Jacques … Dormez vous? Dormez vous? Sonnez les matines, sonnez les matines…Ding dang dong, Ding dang dong…Frere Jacques, Frere Jacques, Dormez....
{sees Adi standing, watching} Can I help you?

ADI: Do you mind if I sit here?

VICKY: Free country.

ADI: Ha! That must be nice. *{He sits next to her on the bench}* That was a lovely song.

VICKY: Was it?

ADI: Yes. It's so long since I heard it. *{Silence}* Are you French?

VICKY: No!

ADI: Sorry. I just thought…

VICKY: They teach you it in school. Least, I think that's…yeah – dunno…

ADI: Ah. It just reminds me…. *{looking towards the buggy}* And you care for your baby. Does he look like his father?

VICKY: Hope not!

7

ADI: Ah….sorry.

VICKY: What for?

ADI: For causing you…distress.

VICKY: I'm not… "distressed." Just…his dad's not around,
that's all.

ADI: I'm sorry.

VICKY: And you don't have to apologise.

ADI: I just mean - if it's what you want.

VICKY: Not really. He didn't hang around. His choice.

{silence}

ADI: Can we start again, please?

VICKY: *{half-laugh}* If it's what you want.

ADI: Okay. Can I sing to him?

VICKY: Er…depends.

ADI: Don't worry – it's nice. *{sings ''L'araignee Wincy''
in French}*

L'araignée Wincy monte à la gouttière
Tiens voilà la pluie,
Wincy tombe par terre,
Mais le soleil a séché la pluie…
L'araignée Wincy remonte à la gouttière

VICKY: Well, that was nice. What was it?

ADI: It's about a spider – climbing up a drainpipe again
and again.

VICKY: "Incy-Wincy Spider''? I thought I recognised it.

8

ADI: It's about never giving up.

VICKY: Didn't know they did it in French.

ADI: Voila!

VICKY: You're not from round here, then?

ADI: Is it obvious?

VICKY: Well… you don't meet many…

ADI: Good-looking men?

VICKY: *{laughs}* No!

ADI: You saying I'm not handsome?

VICKY: I'm just saying…

ADI: I'm black?

VICKY: No – you're French. Are you an immigrant?

ADI: Yes. A legal one, though. Don't worry – they won't arrest you for talking to me.

VICKY: Wouldn't bother me.

ADI: Really?

VICKY: Yes. You do what you can to get by, y'know - same for everybody.

ADI: That's nice. I just - wasn't sure…round here...can be a bit…

VICKY: Yeah – but that's just dodgy people, it's not a dodgy place. So…anyone told you to go home yet?

ADI: One or two. But it's…yeah, I'm used to it.

{beat}   My name's Adi.

9

VICKY: Nice to meet you.

ADI: And your name is?

VICKY: I'm not looking for anyone.

ADI: Me neither. It's just…

VICKY: Just what…?

ADI: Well - we're here on a bench in the park…it's a nice day…I just thought…

VICKY: Oh….okay…it's Vicky.

ADI: Vicky?

VICKY: Short for Victoria.

ADI: That's nice.

VICKY: Yeah, right. Thought you weren't trying to pick me up?

ADI: Sorry.

VICKY: Stop apologising!

ADI: *{laughs}* Okay, okay.

VICKY: So - what you doing here?

ADI: In the park? It's so peaceful. The gardens, the lake – watching the old men playing boules.

VICKY: Bowls.

ADI: Excuse me?

VICKY: It's bowls! Got an "s" on the end.

ADI: Free English lesson! Okay. So why are you here?

VICKY: It's where my grandad used to play. Got me an ice lolly, sat me down here *{nods at bench}*. Spent hours watching him and his team - all in their whites… only thing he was interested in – well, that, and the football.

ADI: Ah. In France it's not just old people who play. And you *throw* the balls instead of rolling them.

VICKY: Bit more exciting.

ADI: It can be. But sometimes you can have…too much excitement…. *{beat}*

VICKY: Like home, this. Least, it was when me grandad…y'know…sort of brings it all back, coming here…with the bairn.

ADI: Ben? *{smiles at the baby}* Is that his name?

VICKY: No – it's Georgey. He's my "bairn"…my baby…that's what we call them.

ADI: Sorry, my English is….

VICKY: Yeah - much better than my French. Anyway, I bring him here because…it's special, this place. For me. Might just give him something nice to remember, when he's a bit older.

ADI: Yes – that's important. When you are young there are some things you never forget…

{Vicky is looking for something to say}

VICKY: So, anyway - you're…French?

ADI: No. I grew up there but I was born in the Congo. The "Democratic" Republic of Congo. Ha!

VICKY: *{laughs}* Where's that?

ADI: Africa. It's the second-largest country in the whole continent. Ten times the size of Great Britain.

VICKY: Okay. So…Congo, France…What you doing here? Not the park. Like – what are you doing over here? In this place?

ADI: I sometimes wonder…

VICKY: Did you come here in a boat?

ADI: No! Thank God – but I know people do that. No, I'm not a refugee now. I came to England to work. Look, I was born in the Congo, but France is my home. Do you speak any French? You say you learned it in school?

VICKY: Nah. I can do numbers: un, deux, trois. And "Frere Jacques," obviously. Don't know what it's about, mind.

ADI: What about famous Frenchmen? Thierry Henry? Zinedine Zidane?

{Vicky shakes her head} They were footballers.

{shrugs her shoulders} Or the President? Emmanuel Macron.

VICKY: Nah.

ADI: So, nobody?

VICKY: Nah…Oh - there was one….what do they call him? Daft name… *{searching for it}*…old man with a pipe…Taxi. Taxi? No…Tatty! That's him. Tatty!

ADI: Tatty?

VICKY: Yeah. Old films. Black and white. My grandad used to *wet* himself laughing.

ADI: Jacques Tati! You know Jacques Tati?

VICKY: Is that him?

ADI: Yes! He was a famous French actor. I can't believe it...

VICKY: What?

ADI: I've met someone in England who knows Jacques Tati!

VICKY: Well, I wouldn't say I *know* him.

ADI: No, but you've heard of him. That's amazing!

VICKY: My grandad had one of his videos. Used to watch it with him all the time.

ADI: Can you remember which one?

VICKY: Well...he was at the beach.

ADI: *{excited}* Yes! "Les Vacances de Monsieur Hulot!" It's my favourite!

VICKY: *{laughing}* Well... who'd have thought?

ADI: When I first arrived in France my parents used to play it for me. Because there wasn't much talking...so I could still understand...and just laugh at the things he did. He was *so* funny. Like this...

{Adi stands and launches into an exaggerated impersonation of Jacques Tati, leaning forward and walking up and down with his hands on his hips. Lifting his hat and taking his pipe from his mouth. He sits when he sees the bemused look on Vicky's face}

ADI: Oh God, now I'm embarrassed. Was that stupid?

VICKY: *{laughing}* Don't worry. Highlight of the day, that, man.

13

ADI: But don't you think it's incredible? That we both like Jacques Tati? He must have been dead for years.

VICKY: It was the name, man. I mean - "Tatty!" *{laughs}*

ADI: What's funny about that?

VICKY: Well – "tatty." It's like…y'know….messy. "Bit of a state." Round here, anyway – that's what it means. Just thought it was a daft name.

ADI: Ah…and your grandad. Watching the film actually made him…pee?

VICKY: Eh?

ADI: You said that he…"wet himself" …?

VICKY: No, no – that's just…it's a…a "saying." Something you say that, like, exaggerates things.

ADI: *{genuinely excited}* Ah, right…still…amazing!

{Vicky smiles - a boy runs towards them}

BOY: Adi! Adi!

{he lifts his hand for a high-five} Adi – it is you, isn't it?

ADI: Yeah, sometimes I wish that maybe.…but yes, it *is* me.

BOY: Me dad says you're rubbish. But I think it's just 'cos you don't get the service. And you never get a game!

ADI: Thank you for pointing that out – you're a bright kid.

BOY: How'd you miss that one last week, though? You were, like, almost on the line!

ADI: I know, I know. I'm sorry. The ball just came so fast.

BOY: D'you think we'll go down?

ADI: We'll be fine! I promise.

BOY: Me mam says you should never make promises you can't keep.

ADI: Well, in that case – I promise to do my best. Here *{takes a silver money clip from his pocket, peels off a £20 note and gives it to the boy}* For you.

BOY: Twenty quid - get in! Cheers Adi. You're not as crap as everyone says you are!

{He runs off. Vicky is open-mouthed, staring at Adi. He turns back to face her}

ADI: What?

VICKY: What was that all about?

ADI: Just…a fan.

VICKY: Yeah – I sort of got that. So you're a footballer? Should've guessed. "Billy Big Boots" - chucking money away like that.

ADI: It was only twenty pounds.

VICKY: Only?

ADI: I'm sorry. I…didn't think….

{Vicky stands up to leave}

          Don't go.

VICKY: Got to – left my mam and she needs me. It's complicated. Listen - nice to meet you.

ADI: But…will I see you again?

{Vicky walks away with pram}

Scene 2

Wednesday, early evening. Adi's luxurious sea front flat at the Marina. Adi's agent, Mike, is on his phone and swigging from a bottle of lager.

MIKE: Yeah, yes he is, mate. *Really* desperate. Yeah…yeah, I think they'd go for that. Sounds about right. And both of us would…? Yeah, you scratch mine and I'll…yeah, sweet. Just – let me know asap, okay?

{Adi enters} Look, gotta go. Yeah, leave it with me. Yeah. Bye…bye…bye.

{to Adi}   Okay mate?

ADI: Who was that?

MIKE: Er…just some bloke. Just, er…asking if you want one in black or red. Which do you fancy?

ADI: Black or red? Sorry, I…?

MIKE: Brand new Porsche. Looks the business. Noisy – just how you boys like 'em. The girls love em as well, by the way.

{Mike puts his beer bottle on the table as he speaks. Adi picks it up and drops it in the bin}

What y' doing? That's what I got you a cleaner for. Look, anyway, this Porsche…

ADI: I didn't…

16

MIKE: Yeah, you don't have to thank me. I got your folks a house, remember? When you kindly agreed to take me on as your agent? Thought you'd like something a bit flash? All part of the service.

ADI: But, how did you…?

MIKE: Best not to ask, Adi, y'know? Just…enjoy. And let's go for red, eh? Says more about you.

ADI: But…it's not something I need.

MIKE: And?

ADI: And it's not something I want.

MIKE: You don't make this easy, do you? You know how much you'd pay for a new Carrera? 90 grand.

ADI: Have I paid that?

MIKE: You haven't paid anything, son. Told you. It's sorted. That's all you need to know. Might need you to make a few personal appearances. Kiss up to a few corporates. The usual. I've signed those photos for you, by the way.

ADI: The ones of me? For the fans? They were for *me* to sign.

MIKE: Yeah – they'll never know. Most of them can't read, anyway. Need you to sign this, though.

ADI: What is this?

MIKE: The Porsche. You don't have to read it. I've done that for you. *{hands Adi some papers}*

Just – there, at the bottom. And there. *{whips them away before Adi can read them}*

17

Good boy. It's taxed. I've got you insurance with a mate of mine. I'll get the keys in a couple of days. Then you're away. The world's your lobster.

ADI: But why do I need a car like this?

MIKE: Blacked-out windows, the latest sound system. Goes like shit off a shovel. King of the bloody Road.

ADI: But I only have to get to the training ground. It's two kilometres away.

MIKE: Yeah, and you got the bloody bus once. That worked out well, didn't it?

ADI: It was only one old man.

MIKE: Yeah – and they're the worst. I've told you – keep away from the Great Unwashed. Unless they're…y'know…good looking.

ADI: I did meet a girl.

MIKE: Whoa - what? When? You never said.

ADI: This afternoon.

MIKE: So - what was she like?

ADI: Nice.

MIKE: Nice? What does that mean? "Nice."

ADI: Just – you know…*{shrugs shoulders}*

MIKE: What – blonde? Dark? Small? Biiiiggg? *{gestures with cupped hands}*

ADI: Leave it, Mike.

MIKE: Why? What's wrong with you?

ADI: Nothing.

MIKE: No, come on. What is it with you? Young guy.
Single - in a foreign country. Loads of dosh. Premier League!
You should be enjoying yourself.   You could have any girl you
want. You should be happy!

ADI: It's not as easy as that.

MIKE: No – listen, mate – it is! You want me to fix you up
with someone? Now? Tonight? Just say. I pick up the 'phone,
she's here - 10 minutes max.

ADI: Non…

MIKE: Any girl you want. Who'll do *anything* you want.

{Adi shakes head}

Just think! *{still no reaction – Mike is agitated}* Adi. You're
boring!

ADI: Yeah, yeah…

MIKE: No! Look - I do everything to make you happy. I
get you a transfer. Get you to England. Get you a great deal.
What do you do? You sit there and stare at the bloody sea!

{Adi shrugs his shoulders} That's not why we brought you here.

ADI: And why did you bring me here?

MIKE: Why? Because it's England!

ADI: No – I mean why did I come here? To this club?

MIKE: Because they pay you good money.

ADI: Is that it?

MIKE: And they paid your old club 15 million Euros.
Which no-one else would.

ADI: So why don't they look after me?

MIKE: Eh?

ADI: You spend a lot of money on something, you take care of it, right?

{Mike shrugs his shoulders}

So - why don't they care for me? It's like I don't exist.

MIKE: Adi – it's a job. A bloody good job.

ADI: Huh!

MIKE: Millions of people would love to be you!

ADI: Not if they knew…

MIKE: Knew what?

ADI: How it is.

MIKE: Right. And how is it?

{beat – Adi is staring into the distance}

ADI: It's…not easy.

MIKE: Okay, okay – not easy at the moment. But it will get better.

ADI: Maybe.

MIKE: Course it will. Look – how good was it at your last club? You were scoring goals for fun.

ADI: That was League Two, in France. This is different.

MIKE: Listen, Adi, you're good – you know you are. You know how to stick that ball in the net. You never lose it. I'll have a word about getting you more game time. And remember - this place is only a stepping stone....anyway – don't go saying things like that out loud. About how bad it is.

ADI: What?

MIKE: God, I need to get you some media training...To me - okay, but reporters? No. Or the fans. Cos they put that sort of stuff on-line, and then you're in deep shit.

ADI: They already put plenty on-line.

MIKE: How do you know? You never look.

ADI: I don't – but others do. And they tell me. What they write is evil.

MIKE: It doesn't help that you won't have anything to do with them.

ADI: Why would I want to have anything to do with people like that?

MIKE: I know, I know, but it might just...you know...if they felt you were on their side?

ADI: On the side of who? Of racists?

MIKE: They're not all like that.

ADI: They say: "it's only a few" – but a small amount of many millions is still thousands.

MIKE: Okay, okay but it still doesn't make it easy - trying to sell you, when you don't sell yourself.

ADI: Like on a shelf, in a supermarket? They might have bought me but they can't buy my whole life.

{Mike smiles, sarcastically}

MIKE: Look – why don't I do it for you? The online stuff? Get you your own website. You know how much you can make from those?

ADI: Did you not hear what I said?

MIKE: Yeah – you hate it. Okay. But you don't *actually* have to get involved. You don't even have to look at it. I'll do that – or I'll pay someone to. I can get you a deal. You just gotta say nice things about…I dunno…aftershave or…lager or something…

ADI: But I don't drink.

MIKE: So? You don't have to *like* them – just say you do. Who's gonna know?

ADI: I'll know.

MIKE: Adi, come on! Look…just think – a few grand for every endorsement. Might help pay for that stuff back home you keep talking about…what is it? An orphanage or something?

ADI: Yes, I…I want to do something good, but…

MIKE: I know. Wouldn't be top of my list, but whatever turns you on. And I'd get that one in the papers, eh? I can just see the headlines: ''Saint Adi Dokobu – the Saviour of Kids in the Congo''. They'll bloody love you for that!

ADI: That's not…argh, why is this all so complicated? Look, the fans here – they don't like me. Unless I score.

MIKE: Which hasn't happened much, 'cos you've spent most of your time on the bench. So that might explain?

ADI: Yeah - thanks.

MIKE: Well it's true!

ADI: And why do they still call it a "bench"? They have big padded seats – very comfy ones.

MIKE: That's just…how it was…years ago. When every football ground was a dump and players like you were on a tenner a week. Look, Adi - what did they buy you for? To score goals. You don't score goals – so they're not happy.

ADI: It's not all my fault.

MIKE: They don't care whose fault it is. The result – that's all that matters. The team wins – everyone's smiling. Lose - they want to scream at someone. Not just here – anywhere! France, Spain, Italy. Look, football – it's the greatest game in the world…when you're winning.

ADI: And my team-mates. They all have their "friends": the South Americans, the Europeans. Even the Africans treat me differently because they think I'm French.

MIKE: That's what people do. They stick with what they know – with who they know. Look – the team's shit. That's why they paid big money for you, when other clubs maybe…you know…

ADI: Okay – so the team is no good. So that's why they bought me. But they can still talk to me!

MIKE: About what? Cars? Beer? The new X-Box? Wasted on you! You're not interested. Look - it's the Premier League – it's a platform for you. Doesn't matter who you play for – City, United, Liverpool. Even this lot! It's England. It's on tv around the word! Everyone watches you. Millions and millions of people. It's your chance to be someone.

ADI: *{gets to his feet – agitated}* Yes, but who? Who am I? *What* am I?

MIKE: What are you? Listen – you're a Premier League footballer. You can do anything. You can buy anything. You can have anything – or anyone. Like this girl – what's her name?

ADI: It's…Vicky – Victoria.

MIKE: Okay. Where does she live?

ADI: I don't know.

MIKE: Great! Did you get her number? *{Adi shakes his head}* Adi! Shit - have I taught you nothing?

ADI: She knows Jacques Tati.

MIKE: Who?

ADI: Doesn't matter.

MIKE: Was he…Paris St Germain?

ADI: *{rueful laugh, shaking head}*   No - Monaco…? Midfielder, wasn't he…?

ADI: And she sang "Frere Jacques" …

MIKE: Right – a singer. She's in a band? You were in a nightclub?

ADI: No – she was singing to her baby in the park.

MIKE: The park! Bloody hell. Which one?

ADI: I don't know – the one by the sea. Just…down the road…

MIKE: We'll go look for her.

ADI: No!

MIKE: Come on, get your coat. You take the main gate, I'll go round the back.

ADI: Don't be stupid.

MIKE: Yeah, it is a bit late - first thing tomorrow.

ADI: Mike!

MIKE: Tell you what - I'll call the cops. Special Branch. Find a "nice" girl round here – they could be out there for bloody weeks!

ADI: Mike! Shut up, will you!

MIKE: *{laughing}* Hey! Okay…it's cool, it's cool. So I'll leave this one with you, yeah? Right. Just…make sure you *score* next time, eh?

{Mike's phone rings – he answers it while walking offstage, leaving Adi alone} Sorry – got to take this…Ricky – my man! What a goal that was, son! Yeah, *extra* special. All day - Sky Sports - on repeat. That, my friend, has just earned you an all-expenses-paid trip to the club of your choice…yeah! I know, I know…

Scene 3

The next day - Thursday. Back in the park. Same bench. Same time. Adi is sitting, alone – hoping Vicky will turn up, and miserable because, so far, she hasn't. A teenager approaches.

LAD: All right? It's Adi, isn't it?

ADI: Hello.

LAD: Thought it was you. What you doing here?

ADI: I'm just…out for a walk.

LAD: Right. Just – don't expect to see your lot round here.

25

ADI: My lot? Excuse me?

LAD: Y'know. Footballers. Should be – I dunno – in a casino or something?

ADI: We're not all like that.

LAD: No, but most of you…hey, the lads won't believe this. Can I get a selfie?

ADI: Okay.

LAD: *{takes out a mobile phone and moves in close to Adi}* Smile, man - doesn't hurt!

{Half-smile from Adi. Vicky approaches, with buggy}

ADI: *{Jumps up, before the lad can take his picture}* Hi!

LAD: Woah. That your lass?

VICKY: No!

LAD: Can I get a picture of the two of you? Or the three of you – Adi, is that your bairn?

VICKY: What do *you* think?

LAD: Just asking.

VICKY: Well now you've asked…

ADI: Yes – can you just…

LAD: Aye, all right, all right. Didn't want a picture, anyway. Don't know what you're doing with him, pet. He's shite! Waste of money. Should fuck off back home, mate!

{The teenager runs off. Adi moves to run after him. Vicky stops him}

ADI: Come back and say that!

VICKY: Adi – leave it.

ADI: But…

VICKY: He's not worth it.

ADI: But you can see what I… *{shakes head}*

VICKY: I know – I'm sorry. We're not all like that.

ADI: *{sighs}* Anyway…I was hoping to see you again.

VICKY: Well, I…come here every day – even if it rains.
Nothing much else, is there? I can't go back to work – there's no-
one to look after the baby. Not since my mam…. and the park's
free, so…

ADI: Well - I'm happy you came.

VICKY: And I thought you might be throwing your money
around again.

ADI: *{laughs}* Yes – I'm sorry about that.

VICKY: Don't start that again! So you're a footballer?

ADI: Yes.

VICKY: But…not a very good one?

ADI: That depends who you ask! I was good once, I think.

VICKY: When was that, then?

ADI: When I was in France. I loved it. It was just
so…natural, for me. It was all so easy. From being a boy it was
something I could do well.

When I was out there, playing…everything else just… and I
signed for a club there. And we were good. *Very* good. And my
parents, and my friends, they could come, and I was so happy…
Maybe I should have stayed? But someone saw me

27

there…scoring lots of goals. They made an offer, brought me to England…and that's why I'm here.

VICKY: So what's gone wrong?

ADI: Just about everything. I came knowing no-one. The season was halfway through, so all the team already knew each other and had made friends. The only person I speak to is my agent.

VICKY: An agent. What does he do?

ADI: Looks after me. Tries to run my life.

VICKY: That must be all right?

ADI: No, it's just…he does his best, I suppose. He found me a flat, and now he's buying me a car.

VICKY: Yeah, that must be really bad.

ADI: No…I know it sounds good, but…he does it for the money, you know – not just for me.

VICKY: It's what people do – work, for money…if they can.

ADI: But he's not my friend. He guides so much of my life. But he doesn't know me.

VICKY: You're a footballer, right? Go on Instagram – in half an hour, you'll have a thousand friends.

ADI: I don't do that.

VICKY: Really?

ADI: I just don't want everyone knowing everything about me … some things are private, you know?

VICKY: What about this, though. You don't mind sharing stuff with me?

ADI: This is different. I don't get to talk to many people outside football. Normal people.

VICKY: Normal? I'll take that.

ADI: *{laughs}* No, I just mean…the football here is very different to France. English fans are very… *{searching for the right word}* …demanding. And the things they shout at you and write about you, and that other players say to you…

VICKY: Isn't that what the referee's for?

ADI: No - these players…they're clever. They wait until they're standing next to you - at a corner, a free-kick. Or when they're running past you, as the ball's cleared and everyone is looking the other way. Just a word, a name…

VICKY: "Sticks and stones…"

{Adi looks at her, quizzically}

"Sticks and stones may break my bones, but words will never hurt me." It's an old saying.

ADI: But that's not true.

VICKY: What do you mean?

ADI: Why should you understand? You've never had to live with it – this abuse, the suspicion, that "look" people give you. The way they talk to you. Like that boy. For what? For something I can't control. You say it's "only words". But when you hear those words every day – even when you go out to play football, something which should make me happy…

VICKY: Suppose I'd…never thought of it…

ADI: It's not your world. But it's mine – and the world for people like me. And it's not just words on the pitch…

VICKY: So - shouldn't you be practising? Trying to get better so you can teach them a lesson? Or… trying to run faster so you can keep out of the way?

ADI: It doesn't matter how fast you run or how hard you try. You don't see it coming. And training? We've already finished. We meet, every morning, 10.30. Warm up…jog around the pitch…have a game. Then we go home - two o'clock. I could die of boredom.

VICKY: What do you do all day?

ADI: Sometimes I go for a run on the beach on my own. Or walk – to places like this.

VICKY: What about the rest of them?

ADI: They watch tv. Play golf. Sit with their phones and their games. *{ironic}* It's a great life.

VICKY: I'll swap you. Then you could try living on what I get. After the landlord takes his chunk – there's hardly enough to feed the two of us!

ADI: That must be tough?

VICKY: *{shrugs shoulders}* We manage.

ADI: How?

VICKY: By…doing without things we can't afford. And as long as the weather's all right I can take him for a walk, come here, get a bit fresh air.

ADI: Do you have a car?

{she gives him a look as if to say "you're joking"}

VICKY: No – but there's buses.

{Adi is quiet for a few moments}

30

ADI: Yes I tried the bus, once…. But I could help you.

VICKY: No – you're all right! That's very kind, but we're okay.

ADI: But you don't have much – you said you hoped I'd be throwing money around?

VICKY: That was a joke.

ADI: Ah…another thing I don't always understand.

{beat}

It's just… you do so much more than me, looking after your son, your mother. And…they pay me…they pay me a lot. Not just me - every footballer. At least, the ones in the Premier League.

VICKY: Well, it's *such* an important job...

ADI: Thousands of people watch us, you know – millions, around the world.

VICKY: Yeah, but – it's football, right? Kicking a ball around?

ADI: I know, I know. The money is not right.

VICKY: I'm sort of wishing I'd never started this…

ADI: I know. I feel bad about it…

VICKY: Go on then – you've gone this far. Embarrass yourself.

ADI: Okay. I'm not proud of it. They pay me…seventy thousand pounds.

VICKY: Well – good for you. That's all right.

{beat}

ADI: A week.

VICKY: A week? Sh…it! That's, like…ten thousand pound a day?!

{Adi looks at her, apologetically}

Every day? Even now? You've just earned, what, a hundred quid - sitting here, talking to me!

{Adi shrugs his shoulders}

VICKY: That's… *{she's lost for words}*

ADI: I didn't ask for it. Mike, my agent…

VICKY: That would keep me and Georgey and me Mam, like…forever! What you earn in a week…for playing football? And for being rubbish?!

ADI: Hey - I'm not that bad! And the money had nothing to do with me. I told you - Mike did the deal.

VICKY: Sorry Adi, you're a nice guy an' all that, but you think you've had it tough? Have you ever had a proper job? Like – a real one, where you've got to graft? Where they don't run around blowing your nose for you and telling you how great you are? Have you ever gone all day with nothing to eat, because you're saving it for the bairn? Or had to choose between… a pint of milk or keeping the heating on for an hour?

ADI: I'm sorry…

VICKY: And it's not just me. It's the thousands of poor sods who spend their money watching your sad team every week, screaming at you to…put a bit of joy in their lives for 90 minutes.

{Gets up}

Look - I can't handle this. You're a millionaire, and you're sitting here feeling sorry for yourself?! If you're *that* miserable go and buy yourself a life! *{she walks off}*

ADI: Please, Vicky! Don't go…Vicky – I'm sorry. I'm….sorry….

Scene 4

Thursday evening. Vicky's flat. She is there with her friend, Ange, who is doing Vicky's hair.

ANGE: And he's a footballer?

VICKY: Yeah.

ANGE: Like – a proper one?

VICKY: Eh?

ANGE: Plays for a team? Not just...kicking a ball around with his mates?

VICKY: Don't think he's got any mates.

ANGE: You know what I mean.

VICKY: Yeah - he plays for the Town.

ANGE: You're kidding?! What do they call him?

VICKY: Adi.

ANGE: Adi? Adi what? *{picks up phone to look him up on-line}*

VICKY: Dunno

ANGE: You didn't ask him?

VICKY: No.

ANGE: And you've not looked him up? Is he on Twitter?

VICKY: He says he doesn't do it.

ANGE: You are kidding, of course? *{flicking through her phone}*

VICKY: No. He's very...down to earth.

ANGE: Down to earth? And he's a footballer? Yeah, right! So how many dates have you had?

VICKY: They weren't dates – I met him in the park.

ANGE: In the park! What – behind the bushes?

VICKY: Shut up! It's not like that.

ANGE: But you've met him twice? So that's, like, two dates more than you've had in the last, what? *{points towards baby}* Two years?

VICKY: Told you! They weren't dates. We just...sat and talked.

ANGE: Exciting! So - what was he like?

VICKY: Dunno. Just...a bit lost, really. He had nowt to do.

ANGE: Ha! Join the club.

VICKY: And he's a long way from home.

ANGE: Which is?

VICKY: The Congo

ANGE: Woah! Where's that?

VICKY: Africa. And it's ten times the size of Great Britain.

ANGE: Africa? Right. So he's....?

VICKY: Yeah.

34

ANGE: God, he's brave – coming here. 'Cos you know what people say?

VICKY: Yeah, but not all people. Not the ones I care about.

ANGE: And all I care about is you being happy. So – great.

VICKY: Well it's not got that far. Not yet, anyway.

ANGE: Alright. But…being a footballer…he must be minted? Which would help?

VICKY: Ha!

{Ange finds his profile online}

ANGE: Right! Here he is: Adi…how d'you say this? Doku…Doko…?

VICKY: Dokobu.

ANGE: Ha! Thought you hadn't looked him up? Here - that him? *{shows phone to Vicky}*

VICKY: Yeah, that's him. Rubbish picture, mind.

ANGE: Rubbish player, judging by the comments. Ooh, they don't like him, do they?

VICKY: What are they saying?

ANGE: Er…let's have a look: "waste of money… get rid… Hang on – this one says: "couldn't hit a cow's arse with a banjo!"

VICKY: Eh?

ANGE: Yeah! Why would *anyone* want to hit a cow with a banjo?

VICKY: Weird.

ANGE: He looks all right though – even if it is a crap photo.

VICKY: Yeah – he's better looking than that.

ANGE: And – obviously – like I said - he's loaded?

VICKY: Don't.

ANGE: Did you not ask him?

VICKY: He didn't want to tell me.

ANGE: 'Course he didn't.

VICKY: It's ridiculous.

ANGE: I'm liking the sound of this! Ha'way.

VICKY: All right…. Seventy grand…

{Ange's mouth drops open} A week.

ANGE: You – are – joking!

VICKY: No.

ANGE: Bloody hell!

VICKY: I know. It's…horrible.

ANGE: Er – not the word I'd use.

VICKY: Which is?

ANGE: Fantastic? Amazing? Jammy?

VICKY: Jammy?

ANGE: Aye – for you! You're the lucky cow he's picked up!

VICKY: Woah! Hang on. One - he's not picked me up. And two - "lucky cow"? Nothing lucky about meeting a decent lad and finding out he's from a completely different world.

ANGE: Sounds all right to me! Not sure why he'd be hanging round a park, mind. Where were the rest of the team?

VICKY: I don't know – down the bookies or playing golf or something. That's why he was…"hanging around.''

Anyway…I've blown it.

{Ange looks at her} Big style.

ANGE: What have you done now?

VICKY: My fault. I lost it with him. I went on a bit of a rant about him feeling sorry for himself. I couldn't help it. He just…really wound me up, you know? He didn't mean to. He wasn't…it just made me feel… He'd been waiting, for me, as well.

ANGE: Waiting?

VICKY: On the bench. Said he hoped I'd come back.

NAGE: Sounds promising.

VICKY: Yeah. But I told him to… Oh, sugar.

ANGE: Ah…

VICKY: All that money…and he's still miserable.

ANGE: You want to see some of the ones I get – the way they go on. Loads of money, but if it's not their hair or their weight or their dog or their kids, it's their bloke or his mam. Sometimes, when I've got the scissors… *{she gestures with the scissors}*

VICKY: Careful!

ANGE: I feel like taking a big chunk off the top…accidentally on purpose, you know? Just to give them something proper to whinge about.

{Vicky smiles} Although just there *{Ange points scissors towards Vicky's jugular vein}* That's the spot, isn't it?

37

VICKY: Hey, man!

{Ange laughs, and takes scissors away}

ANGE: Anyway. You're not going to give up, are you? Just 'cos he's loaded!

VICKY: But I've done all right, haven't I? On my own?

ANGE: Well…you're surviving.

VICKY: We're okay, me and Georgey and me Mam - we manage.

ANGE: Yeah – you manage.

VICKY: So what's wrong with that?

ANGE: You get by – and what else do you do?

VICKY: Take him out…go to the beach…go down the park.

ANGE: Wow – sorry, can't keep up!

VICKY: Look, it doesn't sound much, but you try it! You try looking after a kid on your own! With me mam as well…

ANGE: I know – sorry Vic. Look…you do your best. Course you do. But – just think. You could be in a mansion, with a butler, a nanny for Georgey, and…and…someone doing your hair every week – doesn't *have* to be me, but, y'know…

VICKY: I know, I know.

ANGE: So - what the *hell* is your problem?

VICKY: Well…course I've thought about it, but…I just…do I need this right now? Y'know – I've been there. And… it's not great.

ANGE: Yeah – but sometimes it can be! Okay, your last one wasn't…

VICKY: Exactly. And my dad…

ANGE: Look – they're not all like that! Can't think of a good example right now, but…

VICKY: See. Maybe it's just not the right time?

ANGE: But you've just had to give up your job – there couldn't be a better time.

VICKY: I wouldn't do it just for the money! What do you think I am?

ANGE: Well - I think you're a single mam who's out of work, trying to care for *her* mam and her bairn - and who could do with a bit of looking after herself.

VICKY: That's really going to impress him, that.

ANGE: Listen – you've done the hard bit. He was there, waiting for you…he likes you.

VICKY: But he's way out of my league.

ANGE: Hey – don't do yourself down. You're a bloody great catch – for any bloke. And anyway, sometimes in football the little team wins - even I know that! Give yourself another chance, man, Vic – you deserve it. And, also, next time you're down the food bank, looking for a tin of beans and a pack of nappies, just think what life *could* be like…

Scene 5

Next day - Friday, late morning. Stage left, Mike is on the phone, doing a deal. Stage right, Vicky is on the phone, talking to the Department of Work and Pensions.

39

MIKE: Yeah, you know what he can do – even if he hasn't done it much lately. He's got time on his side, mate. He's quality, he's still young and at that price it's an absolute steal. So, who do you need to speak to at your end?

VICKY: The Benefits Office? Yeah, look, I'm due in at 10 but I can't make it. I'm really sorry, but I've got my baby and he's not great today and there's no-one I can leave him with – I've got no family who can help and my friends are all busy…

MIKE: Well we all are, mate. Window shuts in a few days – that's why we need to do this *now*. If we can just maybe sweeten it a *tiny* bit more. Because it's a big one, yeah? And, if we can't do it now, how soon?

VICKY: I could maybe make it later this afternoon, or tomorrow – or as soon as he's better. Because I know it's serious…yes, I know, I know…and the name's Vicky – Victoria – Sanderson. This won't affect my payments, will it?

MIKE: It certainly will, mate – it'll do both of us proud. And yes, you cheeky bastard - my own granny would cost you a *lot* more than that if I did sell her! And, er… up front with the payments, as always, please – you know what happens if you break the rules…?

VICKY: You're going to *sanction* me? But I *had* to leave my job…because of my baby…because my mam's poorly and there's no-one to look after him. And I thought it would be alright. I don't believe it!

MIKE: Neither do I, mate - but they're desperate. And he *is* very good, y'know? Despite….well… Anyway, just checking you're got the right account? Not the one over here – the *Zurich* one… And I'll make sure there's not a zero missing, don't you worry! So when do you think we'll hear from them?

VICKY: Ninety-one days! But…what am I going to do? I've got a baby – he's only nine months. And there's my mam - there was nothing else I could do. I *had* to leave – and *you* said it would be all right. Well *someone* there did. And what about the rent? If I've got no money, how do I pay that? I could lose my flat. What'll I do then?

MIKE: Find another one, like I just have. Yeah, midfielder - 18. Great left foot. Absolutely nothing upstairs - the lights are on but no-one's at home! Speaking of which - he'd need the place fully-furnished, so he can move in as soon as he gets there, okay? Got to keep them happy. Got to keep *us* happy, eh? So, let's get this done. Top man. As always, an absolute pleasure doing business…

Scene 6

Friday afternoon. Vicky is back on the bench. Adi runs in.

ADI: Vicky! I'm glad you're still here. Training was late and…are you okay?

VICKY: I can't believe it.

ADI: What? What is it?

VICKY: The bastards. It's not fair!

ADI: Who are they? What have they done?

VICKY: I've been sanctioned.

ADI: What?

VICKY: For three months. Three months!

ADI: I'm sorry, I don't…

VICKY: They stop your money - the government. For three months. Because I gave up my job – because I *had* to. Cos when mam took ill there was no-one to look after Georgey, so I *had* to

41

leave. But they say, apparently, that wasn't a good enough reason. That I should have paid someone to look after him. But that would have left us with nothing. I just…aw, shit!

{Adi puts his arms around her}

ADI: Come on.

{He comforts her, and they look each other in the eye for a moment before Vicky draws away, slightly embarrassed}

VICKY: Sorry, sorry. I shouldn't be lumbering you with all this.

ADI: No – please, don't worry. Is there anything I can do?

VICKY: No – I'll be okay. Just got to sort myself out.

ADI: Are you sure?

VICKY: Yeah. But…thanks.

ADI: Because if it's money…?

VICKY: No, seriously.

ADI: But what will you do?

VICKY: I'll…find something…sorry…it was just the shock. Just been on the phone to them...had to get out of the flat. I shouldn't have…

ADI: If you're sure…

VICKY: Yeah, yeah…I'll be fine…

{beat}

ADI: Look, yesterday…

VICKY: I'm sorry.

ADI: What?

VICKY: For having a go at you.

ADI: It's okay.

VICKY: No, no, it isn't. It's just…sometimes…everything just… *{can't find the words}* Anyway, I'm glad you came back. I didn't mean it, you know…the money thing. Not your fault, I suppose…

ADI: I know. It was a shock to me. I play because I love it – most of the time. But the money…crazy…

VICKY: Yeah…money drives me crazy, as well.

ADI: So what will you do? If they won't pay you?

VICKY: I don't know. But I *will* find something. I always do. You have to, else… *{shrugs shoulders}*

ADI: And I can't help you?

VICKY: You are. By being here. Shoulder to cry on…literally.

ADI: I can stay as long as you like – it's Friday.

VICKY: What's special about Friday?

ADI: There's a game tomorrow.

VICKY: Ah, right. Shouldn't you be training?

ADI: We did that this morning. At least, we ran around the pitch a few times. They don't want us injured, before the match. So the rest of the day we just…sit around.

VICKY: Right. Busy day, then! Hard life.

ADI: It *can* be hard, you know? With the tv, the media. And the fans - writing things on the internet.

VICKY: Ignore them.

ADI: I do! Or, I try to. But it doesn't stop them. You know, someone said I should ''go back to the jungle.'' And they don't even know I did live there once....

VICKY: You lived in a jungle?

ADI: Forget it.

VICKY: But...?

ADI: It's why I like it here. Because...it's so different.

VICKY: Here?

ADI: Yes. With the sea outside my door. It's lovely... I wake up and hear the seagulls.

VICKY: Yeah – they wake me up sometimes! Right racket.

ADI: No – it's nice. And I watch the boats go out, and...they are free to go where they please.

VICKY: They used to build ships here, you know? Massive ones. My grandad used to work on them. The shipyards went right up the river, past where the ground is.

ADI: I've never seen them.

VICKY: All gone. Closed, years ago. The jobs went. So the money went, and the place just, sort of...curled up and died. Starting to get back on its feet now, like. But the only thing anyone cares about round here is your football team!

ADI: I know. Forty thousand fans in the Stadium every week – and we're not even very good!

VICKY: And haven't been for years!

ADI: Have you ever been?

VICKY: Yeah, a few times. With my grandad.

ADI: Did you like it?

VICKY: I liked the chips at half-time. But the fans get so excited, don't they? Because it's their team, their town. Like it's a part of them out there, y'know? And it's not, is it? Not really. It's players from everywhere. No real connection. I bet you'd never heard of this place before you came here.

{Adi nods} So – why'd you come?

ADI: Well, it's England. It's the Premier League. It's "the best in the world." Switch on the tv, anywhere in Africa - you can watch English football.

VICKY: So it was…your "dream", was it?

ADI: It was…a way out. *{beat – Adi looks away}* Football was a way out.

VICKY: From what?

ADI: *{shrugs}* Look…do you want to come tomorrow?

VICKY: What?

ADI: To the match, to see me play. As my guest.

VICKY: That's lovely - but I'm off chips now!

ADI: You'd be well looked after. There's a lounge, with a bar…everything's free. And there's food. Good food - not just chips. And a TV - you wouldn't even have to watch the match if you didn't want to!

VICKY: Well *that'd* be a bonus! *{laughs}* But…no, I can't – I've got nothing to wear.

ADI: So?

VICKY: You're kidding! Have you not you seen them? The WAGS.

ADI: Wags?

VICKY: Wives And Girlfriends. It's what they call them – the ones who hang around footballers. All the latest gear. Spray tan, hair done, new nails – just to go to the match.

ADI: Ah…yes. Some of them are very…persistent.

VICKY: Yeah – 'cos being with a footballer gives them their five minutes of fame. Gets them in the papers. Picture on Instagram. Makes them into something.

ADI: But you're not like that. I just think you're…a good person.

VICKY: Thanks, Adi, that's lovely. But…I've got to see me mam. And there's no-one to look after Georgey.

ADI: Could you not pay…? Sorry, stupid…I mean, I could pay for someone.

VICKY: Thanks, but…I'm not a charity.

ADI: It's not for charity – it's for you.

VICKY: I know, but…God, this is really difficult…I'm trying to make my own way, y'know? Trying to make things work. Just to prove to…well, to myself, as much as anyone.

ADI: You're so brave.

VICKY: Huh! Not by choice. *{gets up to leave}* But that's nice of you. Look, I got to go. Thanks… for being here. And I'm guessing… you won't be here tomorrow?

ADI: No. Three o'clock – I'll be at the Stadium.

VICKY: Yeah. Well…you just show them what you're worth…

ADI: À bientôt.

Scene 7

Saturday afternoon. Vicky is in the kitchen of her flat. Ange shouts to her as she enters.

ANGE: Hiya!

VICKY: Shh! You'll wake the bairn – he's just gone down.

ANGE: Shit! Sorry, sorry…hey are you all right?

VICKY: Don't start me off.

ANGE: No, hey, c'mon. There's something wrong, isn't there?

VICKY: I've been sanctioned – three months.

ANGE: They can't do that!

VICKY: They can – and they have. It's come in writing now. *{shows Ange the letter}*

ANGE: What for?

VICKY: For giving up my job.

ANGE: But that was to look after Georgey.

VICKY: I know. They said it should be fine, but now it's not, apparently.

ANGE: Bastards. So what you gonna do?

VICKY: You can appeal – but there's so much stuff to fill in and it takes ages. So, in the meantime…God – who knows? I can't believe it. It's like they're deliberately try to finish me off.

ANGE: Hey, c'mon *{hugs her}*

VICKY: Every time I try to make a go of something…

47

ANGE: I know.

VICKY: The job, the bairn, then my mam – now this.

ANGE: If they knew what it's like…

VICKY: It's torture!

ANGE: Look, if there's anything you need…

VICKY: I know, yeah, thanks.

ANGE: Anything. I mean it. Might feel like the end of the world, but it isn't. It's three months. We'll find a way. And - there's always your footballer…?

VICKY: Aw, yeah – that's the other thing. The match…I could've been there.

ANGE: Today? Now?

VICKY: Yeah.

ANGE: How come? Did he ask you?

VICKY: Yeah.

ANGE: Don't tell me you said no? {*Vicky looks at her*} Aw, man! You know the other day? I said you were a lucky cow?

VICKY: Yeah?

ANGE: Make that "a daft cow"! What's wrong with you?

VICKY: I don't like football.

ANGE: And?

VICKY: I know…he said I didn't even have to watch.

ANGE: Really?

VICKY: Said I could stay in the bar.

ANGE: Sounds all right!

VICKY: And it was all free.

ANGE: What! So, if you didn't fancy it, did you not tell him you had a mate?

VICKY: Listen – I think that's him…

{she turns up the radio commentary}

RADIO: Town really struggling to get to grips with this one. Just not quite at the races this afternoon. They just need a bit of a lift from somewhere…And could this man give them it? Substitute Adi Dokobu. Not been his year so far, since his big-money move from the French club, Nimes, back in January. A lot of fans asking why they spent so much on a player who hasn't really made a difference. But he's up to the edge of the box now, there's a chance here, and – oh, what a strike! Arrowing its way into the top corner! Dokobu – only his third goal since he moved to the Premier League. His first of the season! It gives Town the lead. Incredible! It's taken a while, but that shows what he can do! And he's giving the crowd a "V for Victory" sign – bit premature, that. They haven't won yet. Still a long way to go in this game. But he's come off the bench with a terrific goal, and maybe – just maybe - the Congolese striker is finally paying back some of the millions the club spent on him…

VICKY: Get in! Adi scored! He scored a goal! Isn't that amazing?

ANGE: Adi! Adi! Adi! Adi!

VICKY: Keep it down, man - Georgey!

ANGE: Sorry…sorry…

{fade down sound. Vicky and Ange dance around, celebrating - silently}

VICKY: God, he'll be so happy. Listen to the crowd. They love him now, don't they? Yeah…yeah…and I could have been there…aw, man…

{Switches off radio} They'll probably carry him off the pitch – now he's a Super Star. Straight to a bar somewhere. Fill him full of booze. Then on to a club full of girls – they'll be his friends now…aw, Ange - I should've been there.

ANGE: So he came back yesterday – to the park? How was it?

VICKY: It was…nice.

ANGE: Ha! Bloody thrill-a-minute, this!

VICKY: No, look – he just likes to talk. And he said he lived in a jungle.

ANGE: What?

VICKY: I know.

ANGE: And he's a footballer?

VICKY: Yeah. I mean, he doesn't live there now, obviously.

ANGE: Did he not explain?

VICKY: No.

ANGE: And you didn't ask him?

VICKY: Seemed like he sort of wished he hadn't said it. So I didn't push it. He offered to help, as well, with the sanction thing.

ANGE: Great. And you…? Aw, Vic, no!

VICKY: It's not right.

ANGE: I can't believe you.

VICKY: And I actually like him. But I couldn't just take his money.

ANGE: Open goal – and you blew it.

VICKY: My head's all over the place.

ANGE: Look – you might still be okay. What time is it? Ten past four. Doesn't finish 'til about five. Get yourself up to the ground and wait for him. I'll stay with Georgey – he's no bother.

VICKY: How desperate d'you think I am?

ANGE: Er – do you want me to answer that? *{Vicky laughs}* It's your big chance!

VICKY: I know…I know…it's just…I don't know what I want.

ANGE: Well…that's okay. But it's not always what you want. Sometimes it's…what you need.

VICKY: But…

ANGE: Listen – I'll look after him. *{points upstairs}* You – lipstick on. I'll ring for a cab. And I'll pay for it – my treat.

VICKY: And what about my mam?

ANGE: She'll be all right – me and Georgey, we'll pop in.

VICKY: You sure?

ANGE: Yes. Are you?

VICKY: *{hesitantly}* Yes.

ANGE: Well get a shift on.

VICKY: What if he doesn't see me? I mean – there'll be crowds outside.

51

ANGE: Well, m'darling – that bit's up to you. Ha'way -
game on!

Scene 8

Saturday, outside the ground, after the game. Mike is on the phone, pacing up and down, taking several calls at once.

MIKE: Yeah – it was a great goal, wasn't it? And he
does that all the time in training, y'know…? I promise you. I've
seen it *so* many times – but the keeper didn't, did he! Absolute
bloody rocket. Past him before he moved…yeah, the French
national side are looking at him – but you didn't get that from me,
okay…? Yeah, I know he's hardly played, but they know how
good he is. Just big him up, will you…? All over the back page,
yeah, that's good. And I'll let you know first – of course I will…

{looks at phone} Sorry, got to go…   *{switches calls to another
agent}* Thought it might be you.…yeah, well you should have
wrapped it up sooner, shouldn't you? There's a *lot* more interest
now…yeah, well don't blame me! Yeah, yeah…we *did* have a
deal – but that was yesterday.…yeah, and I'm sorry – but you
know the score…

{a steward enters, guiding a teenage player towards Mike}

Yeah, yeah – oh, that's *very* nice…and the same to you, mate.

{Mike ends the call} Arsehole…

STEWARD: Mr Mulligan – this is Darren.

MIKE: *{taking the boy by the arm and leads him to one side}*
Thanks mate. I'll see you right. Darren? Great to meet you.

Heard a lot about you, son. You've probably heard a lot about me?

Mike Mulligan – I look after some of the top stars in the Premier League. And a few shite ones as well, but we won't talk about them…! *{laughs} {Mike puts his arm round the teenager and leads him to one side, chatting as Vicky arrives}*

VICKY: Hi. Is this where the players…?

STEWARD: Sorry pet – can't go past here.

VICKY: I know. Sorry…I just want to catch one of
them.

STEWARD: Ha! Join the queue.

VICKY: No. It's okay - he knows me.

STEWARD: Who's that, then?

VICKY: Adi. Adi Dokobu.

STEWARD: Oh! Popular lad…at last.

VICKY: What d'you mean?

STEWARD: Been a waste of space since we bought him.

VICKY: Bit harsh.

STEWARD: You seen him play?

VICKY: No. But he scored today?

STEWARD: Yeah – and suddenly, they all want to meet him.
Funny that. You're about the tenth lass who's asked for him.

VICKY: Really?

STEWARD: Aye. Makes a change. Been calling him worse than muck all season. Comes on, scores a goal, now he's "Boy Wonder". Surprised he's still here, to be honest.

VICKY: Why? Where should he be?

STEWARD: Some team where he might fit in a bit better, you know? Not really working for him, here. Been on the bench all season.

VICKY: But he's only been here a few months.

STEWARD: Yeah, but you can tell – with some of them. If it doesn't happen for them straight off… *{shrugs shoulders}*

VICKY: But…where would he go?

STEWARD: Dunno. There's always someone who'd take a chance on him. Maybe not in the Premier League, but…Europe somewhere?

VICKY: But he likes it here – by the sea.

STEWARD: Ha! You a football fan?

VICKY: Not really.

STEWARD: Thought not. 'Cos that's not how it works, pet.

VICKY: If they'd just give him a chance.

STEWARD: To be fair, he's had plenty – just hasn't stuck them away.

VICKY: I didn't mean like that. I meant…if they got the chance to know him…to *really* know him, like I do.

STEWARD: Aye? And how do you know him, if you're not a fan?

VICKY: Well, we met…on a park bench…

{Mike hears this and realises who Vicky is}

STEWARD: Right.

VICKY: And…and he likes Jacques Tati.

STEWARD: Jack Tatty? Was he at Chelsea?

VICKY: No! Look, sorry, but can you get a message to him?

{Mike intervenes. He speaks first to the steward}

MIKE: Er – I'll take this one, mate, you're okay, you're okay. *{to Vicky}* Sorry love, he's *really* busy right now, y'know? They all want to talk to him. Gary Lineker's putting him on the box, and there's the papers and the radio. So…yeah, *really* sorry but, not tonight, eh?

VICKY: I just need to let him know I'm here. Cos he asked me to come to the match, and I didn't…and I should have…and I wish I'd…anyway, I'm here now. So if you could just…please…

MIKE: Sorry darling, were you not listening? He's *really*, *really* busy. He scored the bloody winner.

VICKY: I know – I *was* listening. And I know it's important – but so's this.

{Mike takes Vicky by the arm and leads her to one side}

MIKE: Look – I'm trying to do some important business here. *{shouts over his shoulder}* Just be a second, Darren! Who did you say you were?

VICKY: Vicky.

MIKE: And you're the one he met in the park?

VICKY: Yes – that's me.

MIKE: Bloody hell. Look, love, do us a favour, eh?
We've got big things planned. He can't be hanging around with
the likes of you.

VICKY: What?

MIKE: In a bloody park! What if The Sun gets hold of
that one – just think what they could do with it.

VICKY: But…he likes me. He asked me to the match.
His guest.

MIKE: Well he never said – and he tells me
everything… Listen love, I made this kid who is. I picked him up
in France when no-one else would touch him. I could *see* how
good he was gonna be. Now – surprise, surprise - they all want a
piece of him.

VICKY: I just need to…

MIKE: Yeah - I know exactly what you need to do now,
love – and that's go home. Like a good girl. Because *I* decide
what Adi does – what car he drives, what house he lives in…I
even tell him what to have for bloody breakfast. He doesn't need
any more help, thank you very much.

VICKY: But I know he'd want to see me.

MIKE: You don't give up, do you? Look – I'll make it
easy for you, but only because I'm a nice guy… How does ten
grand sound?

VICKY: What?

MIKE: To go away and don't bother him again – and
swear you won't tell anyone about the bloody park.

{Vicky is open-mouthed} Ten k… *{still no response from Vicky}*

I don't believe this – okay, you're killing me…twenty! You look
like the sort of girl who could do with it. But you stay away from

my boy, you stay away from that bloody bench, and you never speak to Adi again. Okay? Final offer, love…twenty grand…take it or leave it…

End of Act 1

Act 2

Scene 1

Sunday afternoon. Back on the park bench. Vicky has been there a while and has just stood up to leave when Adi runs towards her.

ADI: Vicky!

VICKY: *{Sitting down again}* Oh. Hi. Didn't think you were coming.

ADI: Sorry, I couldn't get here quicker. My agent was calling.

VICKY: I bet he was.

ADI: Are you all right?

VICKY: What did he say about me?

ADI: About you? He doesn't know you.

VICKY: Oh, he does. And he made it very clear what he thinks of me. After the match, on Saturday – cos I came to the ground. I came to see you. And he was there…

ADI: You came to the stadium? I didn't know…

VICKY: And he offered me…20 grand.

ADI: What?

VICKY: To stay away from you. Not to tell anyone we'd ever met. Basically, trying to buy me off.

ADI: I don't believe it. How could he do that?

VICKY: Did you tell him – about me being sanctioned?

ADI: No – no, of course not. I would never tell him that.

VICKY: 'Cos he seemed to think I needed it. Which I do, of course…

ADI: But you didn't take it? *{Vicky shakes her head}* Sorry, of course you didn't – because you're here. I don't know what to say. But Mike – he's supposed to be on my side. When I see him…

VICKY: No, look, Adi – don't do anything stupid …I know what he's like. I've met his type before. Y'know – thinks money can buy you anything. He probably thought he was doing you a favour.

ADI: I can't believe it…

VICKY: Seriously…forget it. Sorry I couldn't hang around yesterday. He just…blew my mind. I'm just happy you're here. Y'know…you being a superstar.

ADI: So you heard I scored?

VICKY: Yeah - just as I put the radio on.

ADI: That's amazing. Do you know what I did – on the pitch, to celebrate?

VICKY: Did you do a daft dance? Pull your shirt over your head?

ADI: No – I made a sign. Like this *{makes "V for victory"* *sign}.*

VICKY: Oh, yeah – they did say something.

{beat}

ADI: It was for you.

VICKY: For me?

ADI: Yes. It was "V for Vicky"…

VICKY: Really? Huh. Well, thanks.

ADI: No – thank *you*.

VICKY: For what?

ADI: For, just…being here…again…for me. It's so nice – sitting here together…just talking.

VICKY: Ha! Welcome to my world. You'd soon get bored.

ADI: No. I wouldn't.

VICKY: Trust me. You're from a different planet, man.

ADI: It's only France – just across the Channel.

VICKY: No, I mean…your life. It's…not like mine. Not like *anyone* I know.

ADI: You'd be surprised.

VICKY: Doubt it.

ADI: Let me show you.

VICKY: What?

ADI: Let me take you out. Tonight. Just you and me.

59

VICKY: I…I dunno…I mean…What about Georgey? *{points to buggy}*

ADI: There must be *someone* who'll look after him?

VICKY: At five minutes' notice? Told you – my mam can't do it any more.

ADI: You could come to my flat – bring him with you?

VICKY: Never heard of bed times?

ADI: Oh…well, I could come to your house?

VICKY: You're kidding! There's hardly room for the two of us. And I've not washed up. And there's clothes and stuff…

ADI: Don't worry. That doesn't bother me. I've lived in some really terrible places.

VICKY: Thanks very much! I just said it was in a bit of a state – it's not a dump!

ADI: No – I didn't mean…I just meant, I don't care where you live, or *how* you live…I've been through it as well, you know – wondering if this is it…if life will always be as tough.

VICKY: Not tough now, though?

ADI: Look, I just want to spend some time with you…get to know you better…please…

VICKY: I've got nothing in, mind. Unless you like baby food. *{Adi pulls a quizzical face}* It's for him. What's left – I have it. Or there's beans.

ADI: Don't worry – I'll bring something. What do you like? Indian? Pizza? Fish and chips?

VICKY: Fish and chips? *{laughing}* You know how to spoil a girl!

ADI: *{confused}* I don't want to spoil anything! I just want to make things good for you.

VICKY: I know – sorry. It's just, like, if you're English you've got to love fish and chips. If you'd said snails I might have been worried. But yeah – Italian.

ADI: Okay. What time?

VICKY: About eight? It's number three – upstairs flat, just there, straight through the park gates. I'll leave the door so you don't wake Georgey.

ADI: Great. So – that's a date.

VICKY: Oh – it's a date, is it? Thought you weren't trying to pick me up!

ADI: À bientôt.

VICKY: Yeah – what does that mean?

ADI: In French it means: "see you soon…"

Scene 2

Sunday early evening, Vicky's flat.

ANGE: *{singing, Rod Stewart-style, into a hairbrush}* "If you want my body, and you think I'm sexy, come on baby let me know…!"

VICKY: Ange, man!

ANGE: But this it is, isn't it? He's coming round for dinner – or at least "for a nibble!"

VICKY: It's just a meal.

61

ANGE: At the moment?

VICKY: We'll see.

ANGE: Ha! He's in with a chance, then? *{in the style of a football commentator}* "And Adi moves in, he's got the goal at his mercy, surely he can't miss this one?"

VICKY: Shut up, man!

ANGE: "Oh, but Mike's gone over the top - Vicky's pulled out the red card!"

{Vicky throws a cushion at her} "And now Vicky's fighting back! She's sticking the boot in!"

VICKY: Ange, man!

ANGE: What?

VICKY: It's *serious*!

ANGE: Serious? Thought you hadn't got anywhere with him yet?

VICKY: No – I don't mean…look, this whole thing. It's doing my head in. I mean – why's he interested in *me*? Come on…

ANGE: So – this is where I get to list all the great things about you? "What Makes Victoria Sanderson such a Great Catch?"

VICKY: This won't take long…

ANGE: Well, since you're asking: she's kind, she's clever, she's gorgeous, she cares for her mam and her bairn. And she can make a tin of beans last a week! Hey - I could fancy you. Mind, that agent of his clearly doesn't.

VICKY: I know – Mike. What was all that about?

ANGE: It was about twenty grand, actually.

VICKY: I couldn't take it, man.

ANGE: Strictly speaking – not true. I know you didn't want to, and I get it, I've known you long enough – you want to do it all by yourself...but you *could* have taken it.

VICKY: Not if I ever wanted to see Adi again

ANGE: And he said he knew nowt about it?

VICKY: Yeah.

ANGE: And you believe him?

VICKY: I've got to. Otherwise...what's the point?

ANGE: Well – only you two can answer that, darling.

VICKY: He's just...he's not like anyone I've ever met.

ANGE: Cos he's loaded?

VICKY: No, that's not what I mean. He's just... he's got this thing about him. Like...I don't know... like he's got something on his mind.

ANGE: Oh yeah? You know that *is* usually only *one* thing, don't you?

VICKY: No - seriously.   He says he wants to "talk".

ANGE: Well you're in for a cracking night, pet! Have you put clean sheets on, just in case?

VICKY: Trust you.

ANGE: I'm only asking! 'Cos if this "talking" stuff gets a bit, *boring* - y'know – and he starts to nod off...

VICKY: With my chat-up lines he probably *will* - it's been that long...

ANGE: No – you can tell him about how good the new baby buggies are, and how quickly you've got into your old clothes, and how your back's not hurting so much now, and...yeah, I might need to think up some lines for you...

VICKY: Ange man pack it in! You're not funny. It's been ages.

ANGE: You never forget though, do you? It's like riding a bike. Like, a really expensive, top of the range bike!

VICKY: It's all happened so fast.

ANGE: Well, I'll try to make it last a bit longer. I'll take Georgey – he can stay the night with me. Leaves you free to...y'know...

VICKY: Come on, that's not going to happen. I just...haven't got a clue what he sees in me. Just seems, like...too good to be true. *{looks like she is going to cry}*

ANGE: Hey, now, come on, come on. You're a smashing lass. Must be, if I like you! Anyway – only one way to find out what he's after.

VICKY: But...what if it's all for nothing? If he is just stringing me along? I don't think...I couldn't...

ANGE: Hey – ha'way. *{hugs Vicky}* Give him a chance. You've got nowt to lose.

VICKY: Except the tiny bit of dignity I've got left!

ANGE: Look – what's the worst that could happen, eh? He turns out to be a complete bastard – like all the rest.

VICKY: Exactly!

ANGE: So - what have you lost? A few days out of your life.
You've got to go for it.

VICKY: Why?

ANGE: Why? Cos you deserve someone. You care for
everyone else – about time someone cared for you. That's why…

Scene 3

Sunday, early evening, Adi's flat. Adi is talking to Mike.

MIKE: Look, you said she's already got a kid, yeah?

ADI: Just…shut up! It's not like that – I told you.

MIKE: And I'm telling you – she's a single girl. You're a
footballer. A *Premier League* footballer. With more cash in your
back pocket than she'll see in a lifetime. Think about it!

ADI: Look – it's *my* life. What you did – offering her
money…

MIKE: I was looking after you, mate.

ADI: You tried to *buy* her. What *is* that? She's not just
another striker. You think *everything* has a price.

MIKE: Most things, Adi – most things. You've got a lot to
learn, son.

ADI: And so have you! This part of my life, away from
football, is no concern of yours. Okay?

MIKE: But don't you see, how it can look…

ADI: I don't care how it looks. It's how it feels. And for the first time in a *long* time…it feels good.

{beat}

MIKE: Okay…look, Adi – you do what you want, mate. Just - be careful, is what I'm saying.

ADI: I always am.

MIKE: I know I'm always telling you to make the most of things, but don't let her take pictures.

ADI: She won't do that.

MIKE: Not when you're looking. But when your back's turned – she's got her kit off. You in your boxers. Bang! A selfie. Round the world in *seconds*.

ADI: I thought you told me you wanted to see more of me on social media?

MIKE: Don't get clever…

ADI: Anyway, you know nothing.

MIKE: Yeah, but that's where you're wrong, Adi. I know *everything*. That's my job – to know everything for you. To *do* everything for you. I mean – apart from where your lovely lady's concerned.

ADI: Good – so leave me alone!

MIKE: Nah - you don't mean that.

ADI: I do! Why are you always calling me? Checking up on me?

MIKE: Because I'm your agent. Because…if it wasn't for me, where would you be? Still at your old club on five hundred

Euros a week? Not here, on 70 grand? Okay mate. Go home. I'll book your seat, sort your passport. See you. Ta-ra.

{Adi looks fed up} Adi. The world is out there waiting for you. Don't get hung up on one girl. Especially when you don't know what'll happen next.

ADI: What do you mean?

MIKE: It's football – that's all I'm saying. You score a goal, you're a hero. Next week you miss a chance, they spit on you in the street. Then some crazy manager calls and you're off on your travels again!

ADI: But I don't want to go anywhere.

MIKE: You've changed your tune. You've been calling this club worse than shit!

ADI: It's…been a bit better.

MIKE: Well, you scored. That helps. See Match of the Day? Even Shearer was impressed. That goal – everyone'll have seen it. Not just here – all over Europe. Been trending on Twitter – which you'd know, if you ever looked.

ADI: I told you – too many bad things there. Horrible things.

MIKE: Don't start this again.

ADI: And don't you start defending them again!

MIKE: Adi – I'm not defending anyone. They're scum. What they write about you – about all black players…what I'm saying is you can't let it bother you.

ADI: Why? Why should I just ignore it? So they'll go away? It won't happen.

MIKE: Listen – it's wrong. It's shit. Some of that stuff they put on there…it should be illegal – but it isn't. Least, not yet. So you either develop a very thick skin or…

ADI: Yeah – the usual argument.

MIKE: But it works both ways. Don't you see? That goal of yours – wow! Thousands of likes, from all over the world. The power of the Premier League.

ADI: It was only one goal. One lucky shot.

MIKE: Again – don't go telling people that. One striker's lucky shot's another one's brilliant finish. And by the time we've done your new showreel it'll look like you do it every week. Instead of every three months…

ADI: Isn't that…dishonest?

MIKE: It's football – and it's life! It's how things work. Get used to it, Adi. And tonight – just enjoy yourself for a change.

ADI: I just want to show her…

MIKE: Show her what?

ADI: That I care.

MIKE: And why do you care? For this girl? Why's she so special?

ADI: Because…she doesn't care.

MIKE: Nah – you've lost me, mate.

ADI: She doesn't care that I'm a footballer. She's not like the others. They all want something.

MIKE: What about your money? She must want some of that?

ADI: No – she thinks it's not right.

MIKE: Of course it's not right. Nothing in football's right! That's why we love it. That's why people like you and me can live like this! A kid from nowhere and a scally from Birkenhead. Without football, you know what we'd do? We'd steal from the poor instead of the rich.

ADI: So now, we take money from businessmen, who buy football clubs because they want everyone to love them. Who spend billions because – in their world – that is the only way to succeed? By making money?

MIKE: Yeah. And plenty of it comes our way. So what?

ADI: And then, when things go wrong, *they* find out what it's like when the crowd turns against you.

MIKE: But I love you, Adi!

ADI: You love the money I make you.

MIKE: Yeah – and the money I make for you!

ADI: And that's all I have. That's all I have to offer. But Vicky…

MIKE: She'll love it, too, mate. Trust me. In the end – they all do. Ah mate, you have more to offer than that. So tonight – cards, phone…*{laughing}* Condoms?

ADI: Mike!

Scene 4

Sunday 8pm. Adi enters Vicky's flat, just as Ange is leaving. He is carrying a takeaway bag and a bottle of wine.

ANGE: You have a lovely night, pet – and don't worry about Georgey. He's safe with me. *{sees Adi}* Eeh – is this him? Hello, lovely to meet you. I'm Angela.

ADI: Oh, hi – Vicky has told me a lot about you.

ANGE: Don't believe a word. Especially that one about the hen night down the Quayside. Where I got that copper's helmet from I do not know…

VICKY: Ange, man! *{to Adi}* She's just leaving.

ANGE: Ooh, wine – very nice. She doesn't drink, mind – if that's your plan!

VICKY: Ange!

ADI: I don't drink either – I…just thought it was polite.

ANGE: Well, you won't be needing this then *{takes the wine from Adi}* I'll celebrate you scoring that goal.

ADI: Thank you – it's been a long time, so…

ANGE: Well, you never forget, do you? No matter how long it's been, eh…? **{aside to Vicky}** *Very* handsome bike!

VICKY: Just – get out will you!

{bundles Ange out of the door}

ANGE: Lovely to meet you, Adi. Don't do anything…ah, well, you know the rest!

VICKY: Sorry about that.

ADI: Don't worry – she seems nice.

VICKY: She's crackers, actually. But she's my best mate. So, anyway…come on in. This is it. A bit smaller than what you're used to, but it's all right. And it's all I can afford.

ADI: Like I said, I've lived in…

VICKY: Worse?

ADI: I didn't mean it like that.

VICKY: It's okay. I know it's not great.

ADI: I just meant…I don't live in a palace, you know? It's a nice apartment, but…it's not home.

VICKY: So – where's that, then? "Home"?

ADI: I don't know. France, I suppose. Montpellier - where my parents live. The ones who adopted me.

VICKY: So – not the Congo?

ADI: No.

VICKY: Which is where your *real* parents are?

ADI: Where my real parents *were*.

VICKY: So…?

ADI: Look, shall we eat? I'm hungry.

VICKY: Okay. What you got?

ADI: *{dipping into bag}* I didn't know what you liked, so I bought a few things. *{Adi unpacks box after box}*

VICKY: Wow - wasn't expecting this. It's a banquet! *{she starts serving out the food}*

ADI: Well…not really. But - enjoy. You deserve it.

VICKY: Do I?

ADI: Of course. For all the hard work - looking after your mother and your child.

VICKY: Yeah, well…it's what you do, isn't it?

ADI: But not everyone does it.

71

VICKY: Well, that's just the way I am.

ADI: And Georgey's father? You said he'd gone?

VICKY: Yeah, a long time ago. I've no idea where he is. Heard nothing since the day I told him I was pregnant. The look on his face…

ADI: It was a shock?

VICKY: Just a bit. We'd hardly met. Only gone out a few times. Just…one time too many.

ADI: So how did you meet?

VICKY: He came to the place where I worked. He was a driver – doing deliveries. Real charmer. Then, of course, when I found out, and told him… he was gone, just like that. You couldn't see him for dust.

ADI: Did you not try to find him?

VICKY: I rang his work. They said he'd "gone away". Tried his mobile – left messages. Nothing.

ADI: That's so sad – for both of you.

VICKY: Don't go wasting any tears on him!

ADI: And after Georgey was born - did you not try to find him again?

VICKY: What for? He made it pretty clear he wasn't interested.

ADI: So he's never seen the baby?

VICKY: No. And he never will.

ADI: Not even if he comes back to apologise?

VICKY: No! Trust me, he wouldn't do that. And anyway - I do all the work, bring up a kid on my own, give up everything for years, so he can sail back in whenever he wants? You're having a laugh, aren't you?

ADI: A father losing his son? It's nothing to laugh about.

VICKY: He didn't lose him. He gave him away! Couldn't face the responsibility. Left me to do it all on my own!

ADI: But…to not see someone who's a part of you…

VICKY: *{angrily bangs her cutlery down on her plate}* Listen! God, I knew this was a bad idea. Look – what's this all about? Not just the questions, I mean…what are you here for? What are you even doing, talking to me? And all this food and everything. It's a hell of a lot of work, just… for a shag!

ADI: Sorry, Vicky, it's not like that. But family – it means a lot. Please… I'm not just here for…that's not me, believe me. I'm here because…because you and me…I just feel we're the same.

VICKY: You and me? You are kidding! We have absolutely nothing in common!

ADI: Please – Vicky.

VICKY: No! This is stupid.

ADI: Stop, please!

VICKY: Look – I knew this was a bad idea. Just get out, will you, cos this is just doing my head in! I can't take this.

ADI: Vicky – listen to me!

VICKY: No, stop it, man. I can't…

ADI: Please! Just listen…

VICKY: All right, all right. Just…give me a minute!

ADI: Look…you say we're different.

VICKY: Yeah!

ADI: Just listen! *{beat}* We're not *so* different. In many ways we're just the same.

VICKY: And how's that, like?

ADI: You said your father's gone?

VICKY: Yeah.…

ADI: How?

VICKY: What?

ADI: How did it happen? Because I know that feeling too. The pain of losing someone close. It never leaves, no matter how hard you try to push it away…it's with you all the time. So I would like to tell you my story…if you will tell me yours.

VICKY: You really want to hear this? 'Cos it isn't great.…all right. *{beat}* So…my dad liked a drink. And when he'd had a few, he wasn't nice to be around. Like, *really* not nice...to my mam. I was only little, but I knew. I knew enough. I don't know where he went to. Hopefully as far away as possible. I don't even know if he's still alive, and I don't care. I can't let myself care. So, my mam brought me up – like me and Georgey, but with… a bit of help from my grandad.

ADI: And where's he? Your grandfather?

VICKY: *{shakes her head}* Grandad George? He was lovely, my grandad. He would do anything for me. Better than a dad. Just so sad he never got the chance to see…well, that's why I called him Georgey.

ADI: I'm sorry…

74

VICKY: But I had my mam. God, she was fantastic. Always busy. Always smiling. She wouldn't let anything get in the way of helping me and Georgey – and plenty other people. One of the neighbours said: ''Eeh, your mam – y' couldn't knock her down with a stick!'' I loved that. Just so…*her*, you know? I thought she was…unstoppable.

Then about a year ago she got this thing where she lost her voice. She thought it was just a cold, but it went on and on. But they found out, eventually. Motor Neurone Disease. It's really, really horrible. You wouldn't wish it on, like, the worst person in the world.

She used to be in a choir, and she was good. *Really* good. You could always hear her, above everybody else. I loved listening to her sing. It made her so happy. But with this - your muscles just go. Gradually. Day by day. It's like a slow torture. And it got where she couldn't sing any more. So that stopped.

Then she couldn't speak – she has to write everything down. Then she couldn't eat – couldn't keep anything in her mouth. So she's got a tube in her stomach. And now she can't even put her lips together to give me a kiss…

ADI: That's…so sad. Where is she now?

VICKY: Still at our old house for the minute. There's carers coming in every day though. They're lovely – they do everything for her. And I'm there as much as I can now. But it's so hard and she's just…fading away. It's like…everyone in my life just keeps disappearing.

{beat}

ADI: Just like mine. My mother - when she died - she was also surrounded by people.

VICKY: In a hospital?

ADI: No…in our house. *{beat – Adi gets up and walks around}* She was surrounded by soldiers.

VICKY: Soldiers?

ADI: From one of the tribes. I don't know which one. It could have been any of them – so many different countries and gangs fighting the war.

VICKY: You were in a war?

ADI: My country was. I had no choice.

VICKY: What were they fighting about?

ADI: What are wars always about? Money. And oil, and corruption.

VICKY: So why'd they pick on you?

ADI: Why does anyone pick on anyone? Because they think you are weaker. Because they need to be in control. And we were just in the wrong place.

{slowly relives the moment}

That day, there was a group of them – maybe five or six. They came into our house, forced us into the back room – me, my mother and father and my sister…and…they were laughing. They were laughing because they could see how scared we were….and then they took my mother…and they made her kneel…and there was a huge knife…

And my father was next. And what do you think is worse – to have never really had a father, like you? Or to have known and loved him all your life, and then to see him die in front of your eyes? Not a great choice…

VICKY: And your sister?

ADI: My sister? She was beautiful. Her name was Dibenesha. In Congolese that means "blessing". They took us into the bedroom – the soldiers, all of them…and they…

VICKY: God, Adi…

ADI: Each of them…one after the other…while I sat in the corner and shut my eyes and covered my ears, to try to make it all go away…

VICKY: How old were you?

ADI: Ten.

VICKY: So how did you…I mean, how come you're still here?

ADI: Because when it was the last soldier's turn…when the others had gone…he put down his rifle…

And I picked it up, and as he….I pointed it to his head…and with both hands and every ounce of strength……

Dibenesha was lying there, and we heard the soldiers coming back, and she shouted: "Run, Adi - run." And I did. Into the forest. Without her. Without looking back. I ran. And…just like that… my family…gone….

And do you know how that feels? Do you? To be in fear of your life? To run and run and run because if you stop - then your life will stop too? To know your parents are dead and to leave your sister dying. That all you ever knew has just disappeared? Gone. Forever...

For weeks I lived out there, sharing the ground with people I hardly knew, but who kept me safe. Trying to sleep, sleep, sleep, because only then does the pain go away…

77

Scene 5

*Monday morning, in Vicky's flat. Adi and Vicky are under a
blanket. Both still wear their clothes from the night before.
Vicky wakes and eases herself away from Adi, moving towards
the kitchen sink. Adi wakes.*

VICKY: Morning.

ADI: Morning.

VICKY: Sleep okay?

ADI: Yes, thank you. Best for a *long* time.

VICKY: Good...what you said last night...

ADI: Yes. I've...never told anyone before.

VICKY: I know. I'm glad you told me. You didn't even tell
your parents in France.

ADI: They knew I had lost everyone but...I don't
know...it was just too much...and maybe they thought it best not
to ask. I just think...you feel like someone I can trust...like
someone who would understand. Because you've been through
tough times, too.

VICKY: Yeah – but not like that! I mean, wars and soldiers. I
mean...do you still think about it?

ADI: All the time.

VICKY: You can get help you know? Counselling. People to
talk to, who know about this sort of stuff. They can help.

ADI: Thank you. But you are helping. Just by being here.
By listening...

{beat}

VICKY: So...what now?

ADI: Back to work, I suppose. *{Adi takes his mobile phone from his pocket}* Urgh – it's dead. Do you have a charger please?

VICKY: Yeah – just in the wall there.

ADI: Thanks.

VICKY: Want some breakfast? *{she switches on the radio as she fills the kettle}*

ADI: Yes please. Do you have any green tea?

VICKY: Green tea? Nah - I can do brown!

ADI: *{laughs}* Ok – that's fine.

VICKY: Milk?

ADI: No thank you. And no sugar please.

VICKY: Course not.

ADI: I have to look after myself.

VICKY: So, what you up to today?

ADI: Training…what time is it?

VICKY: *{picks up her phone}* Eight-58. Nearly nine o'clock.

ADI: Good – I have an hour *{Adi's phone pings about a dozen times with waiting messages}*

VICKY: Someone's popular!

ADI: Merde.

{Adi hurriedly leaves the room to look at the messages. Vicky turns up the radio}

PRES: Just ahead of the news at nine, a bit of sport from Nick – in football, the transfer window's just about to close, of course, and we're hearing this morning of a big-money deal involving Town's Congolese striker?

COMM: That's right – Adi Dokobu, only signed from the French Second Division club, Nimes, in the last window – he's on the move again, just ahead of the deadline. And he's on his way back to France to join Nice for what they're saying is an "undisclosed fee". We're told the club will get back nothing like the 15 million Euros they paid for him, in January.

PRES: Great move for him, though, Nick?

COMM: Very good move – and it gives the club some much-needed ammunition to go back into the transfer market and find themselves a proven goalscorer. Fair to say Dokobu's not been a great success – that goal at the weekend, when he came off the bench against Tottenham, only his third in the Premier League. But we understand he's heading off to the south of France today for a medical, and if he comes through that he should complete the deal – so he's going home, which can't be bad!

PRES: Yeah – very nice, too. All that sunshine. Got a great life, haven't they? Thanks Nick – more from you in the next…

{Vicky switches off the radio and stares at Adi as he re-enters the room carrying a rucksack.}

VICKY: So…when were you going to tell me?

ADI: I…I didn't know.

VICKY: What!

ADI: Vicky, I swear – I didn't know. Until now – those messages…my phone was dead.

VICKY: You're kidding me?

ADI: No.

VICKY: So no-one told you you're moving to another country? Back to France?

ADI: There was always the chance – the transfer window is still open.

VICKY: But why didn't you tell me?

ADI: Mike - my agent. He does all the deals.

VICKY: And you just go along with him?

ADI: That's how it works. He looks after me.

VICKY: Someone to look after you! Must be nice. I'll try it sometime.

ADI: Vicky…I'm sorry.

VICKY: And what about all this? The food and the wine and everything?

ADI: I just…wanted to be closer to you.

VICKY: Close to me? Yeah, well, that never lasts. All the people in my life just…. Should've known…I should have bloody known!

ADI: *{thinking on his feet}* Look, it doesn't have to end… Vicky, come with me.

VICKY: What?

ADI: Come with me.

VICKY: Where?

ADI: To the south of France. To Nice.

VICKY: Yeah, right!

ADI: I mean it. Come with me.

VICKY: What, now?

ADI: Yes, now. I have to go now – for a medical *{looks at phone}* The flight is at 12 o'clock. Mike can get you on. All I have to do is call him. Please!

VICKY: So - that's three hours to pack up my life here – everything, including the bairn – and just bugger off to France?

ADI: Why not?

VICKY: Get real, man!

ADI: This is real! It's our chance.

VICKY: Our chance?

ADI: To have a life together. For you to start a new one – with me.

VICKY: With someone I only met a week ago? Someone from a different country, who's living a different life…? France, man – told you, I only know "Frere bloody Jacques!"

ADI: I could teach you.

VICKY: Yeah - but what about Georgey?

ADI: He could come too – I could find someone to look after him.

VICKY: But he's mine! That's *my* job! You said yourself – parents, family – that's what matters! And what about my mam? If I go, she's got no-one left. No-one!

ADI: But she's…

VICKY: Yeah, go on – say it. She's dying. Thanks. Thanks for reminding me.

ADI: I'm sorry. I just mean…she wouldn't want to hold you back.

VICKY: And how would you know?

ADI: I'm just saying…any mother would want the best for their child – like you do for Georgey.

VICKY: And this would be the best, would it? Taking him to a foreign country with a man I hardly know? Even if I do…aw, God…

ADI: Please, Vicky…look, I have to go soon – please, come with me.

VICKY: Just get out, man!

ADI: *{pulling on his trainers}* I have to.

VICKY: Yeah, that's right, Adi. Just keep running!

ADI: But this time I don't want to, don't you see? Look. What we had…

VICKY: What we had? What we had was a few chats on a park bench and a…corner shop takeaway!

ADI: But for me…talking to you…like I've never talked to anyone before…because…you mean so much.

VICKY: Yes…it was nice while it lasted, but this is it: The End. It's where it always ends, for me.

ADI: So…you felt it, too?

VICKY: Course I did…! *{they look at each other, neither knowing what comes next. Adi reaches for the rucksack}*

ADI: Sorry, Vicky - I must go…..but…here *{hands her the bag}*…for you.

VICKY: What's this? Leftovers? Cheers!

ADI: No - open it. Look inside. Go on…please.

{Vicky slowly takes out bundles of £50 notes}

VICKY: Jesus.

ADI: It's for you.

VICKY: This my pay-off?

ADI: What?

VICKY: For you – coming round here. Staying the night. Didn't even have to do anything for you!

ADI: No!

VICKY: What do you think I am?

ADI: I'm sorry…Vicky, it's not like that. You're very special.

VICKY: You told me you didn't know you were going.

ADI: I didn't! Please believe me.

VICKY: So what's this?

ADI: I promise – until I saw my phone…

VICKY: So you just happened to come round with a bagful of your loose change?

ADI: Yes. Because you need it more than me. Think what you can do with it. New place, new things - for you and for Georgey…and your mother.

VICKY: I can't.

ADI: You can – please. You must.

VICKY: No! I told you. We're not a charity. It doesn't work like that!

ADI: It's not charity. It's just my way of saying…thank you…

VICKY: For what?

ADI: Just for being there. For listening…

VICKY: I mean, what is this?

ADI: It's seventy thousand pounds. Because…this has been the best week of my life. *{beat – they look at each other and seem about to kiss when Adi's phone rings}*

Look – I have to go… to meet Mike, to sort things out. I'll try to get the flight delayed so you can think about it.

VICKY: It's too much to think about!

ADI: I know…but it's also very simple. If you're coming, meet me – in the park, on the bench. 11 o'clock. I'll be there.

Scene 6

The park bench. Adi is waiting - alone, agitated and looking at his phone. He's about to put it in his pocket when it rings. He looks excited until he recognises the name which appears.

ADI: Mike. Hi.

MIKE: Where are you?

ADI: I'm…out.

MIKE: "Out" as in "out of the flat and on my way to the airport"?

ADI: Sort of.

MIKE: Adi – don't piss me about!

ADI: I'm not.

MIKE: Yes – yes, you are, Adi. Mate, do you know how
hard I've worked for this one? How many hours I've been on the
phone? The favours I've had to call in? I've had to sell my
fucking soul to get you this deal.

ADI: Sell your soul? You actually had one?

MIKE: Don't get smart with me, you little shit. This is what
you wanted!

ADI: And it makes you a lot of money.

MIKE: Yes, it makes me money – course it fucking does.
But it gets you out of here. Away from England. From the fans
who give you shit and the players who give you grief. Isn't that
what you wanted? Isn't that all you've banged on about ever
since you got here? Or have I got it wrong?

ADI: I just need more time.

MIKE: Well you ain't got it, son. They're waiting for you.
There's a car at the airport when you get over there, it'll take you
straight to the ground. They'll have the contract. I've gone over
it – you don't even have to *look* at it. Just pick up a pen, put your
name on it, and it's done – four years, millions of Euros a year.
Just think about that. And it's Nice – it's the south of fucking
France – it's going home! What more do you want?

{beat} Adi!

ADI: Have you got that extra seat?

MIKE: I have, actually. And that was a pain in the arse as
well.

ADI: So how long do I have?

MIKE: You've got an hour. Miss that plane, we're screwed.

ADI: Okay.

MIKE: Where are you?

ADI: In the park.

MIKE: *{off phone}* That *fucking* park! *{to Adi}* Don't move.
I'll send an Uber.

ADI: Okay.

MIKE: Adi…it's the right thing…trust me.

ADI: *{looks up and sees Vicky approaching}* Sorry – got
to go.

MIKE: Adi! Fuck!

*{Adi rings off, puts the phone in his pocket and jumps up to
greet Vicky, who runs towards him}*

ADI: Vicky – this is wonderful!   We'll be so happy, I
promise you. It will be *so* good. The weather, and the lifestyle and
the food and the wine - no, you don't like wine, that's okay. But the
beach, you will *love* the beach, and so will Georgey, and…where's
Georgey?

VICKY: Adi….I'm not coming.

ADI: I don't understand.

VICKY: I couldn't just let you go.

ADI: But why won't you come with me?

87

VICKY: You think I don't want to?

ADI: I'm not going without you.

VICKY: You've got to go. It's your career – your life. And I'll wait for you…to come back for me.

ADI: When?

VICKY: I don't know. When the time's right.

ADI: But why not now? What's wrong?

VICKY: You and me – we both know it couldn't be more right. It's just…God, this is hard…when you love someone, you just…love them, y'know? You can't help it. You'll do *anything* for them. And when someone's looked after you, brought you up – given up everything…

So when *they* need help – you just do it. But this week…meeting you…and just for a second, thinking I might have a different life…I hate myself for that. So I can't leave her, Adi. Not even for you…I'm so sorry.

ADI: I'll phone you, as soon as I land. And I can text you. You come to this bench and we'll speak every day. And…I can teach you French.

VICKY: Yeah – that'll be even harder than playing football!

{Adi's phone pings – he takes it from his pocket}

ADI: My taxi…

VICKY: Don't miss it.

88

ADI: Vicky…wait…before I go… Pouvons-nous embrasser?

{Vicky doesn't understand} It's your first lesson, in French. It means, can we…?

{They look at each other then kiss for the first time}

Goodbye.

{Adi leaves}

VICKY: À bientôt....

The end

CORNERED

by

Jeff Brown

All rights are strictly reserved and application for performance or other uses should be made before rehearsal to Southbank Communications, Kelvey House, Jarrow, Tyne & Wear NE32 5BH. T:07949 765 426. E:Jeffbrowntv@gmail.com.

Permission for the use of television footage should be sought from the relevant owner.

ISBN: 978-1-7397-169-0-5

Published by KELVEY September 2023

Acknowledgements

Cornered is a one act monologue. It was first performed at The Customs House, South Shields, from 6-8 September, 2017, before a short tour of Washington Arts Centre, The Peacock in Sunderland and the Gala Theatre, Durham. It was produced and directed by Paul Dunn at Cranked Anvil, and the part of Davey Corner was played by Steve Arnott.

Cornered is available as an audiobook on iTunes, read by the author, including interviews with David Corner, raising funds for the Foundation of Light, Sunderland.

The play is a dramatisation of a true story with the full co-operation of David Corner.

Reviews

"This funny and at times poignant play finds out what happened to Davey Corner after that fateful day against the Canaries… if you have ever played the beautiful game then you'll appreciate the emotions described in *Cornered*." **North East Theatre Guide**

"Ingeniously crafted…*Cornered* is often played for laughs but has serious moments, too." **Northern Echo**.

'If you haven't seen the play yet you should…I haven't met anyone who has said it was less than very good'… **Ready to Go**

Author's note

I'd like to thank Paul Dunn for spotting the potential of the play, based on a reading at a scratch night at The Customs House; Michael Chaplin for his invaluable script advice, Steve Arnott for his magnificent performance of the central character and most of all David Corner himself, who I sincerely hope has now been forgiven by every Sunderland fan.

Synopsis

Cornered is based on the true story of David "Davey" Corner. On 24 March, 1985, Davey lived out every football fan's dream by playing for his hometown team, Sunderland AFC, in a Wembley Cup final. At 18, it was only the fifth game the tall, ginger-haired central defender had started for the first team. The part he unwittingly played in the 1-0 defeat, which saw Norwich City lift the Milk Cup, changed his life – forever – and became part of Wearside footballing folklore.

Act 1

Scene 1

It's 2018, in the small back office of a local police station… The office has a desk, chair, noticeboard, stationery paraphernalia, kettle, Sunderland AFC mug, coffee jar and milk plus a biscuit tin.

{"Dixon of Dock Green" theme tune}

"Evenin'…"

Actually, that should be: "Evenin' all." Remember him? Britain's nicest bobby!

BBC1. Saturday night telly. About six hours of it, right the way up to "Match of the Day." Fantastic! Kicked off, straight after "Grandstand", with "The Generation Game" – or maybe "Doctor Who". Then it was on. "Dixon of Dock Green" …

Ran for 21 years – 1955 to 1976.

Jack Warner. Old British actor, playing PC George Dixon? No?

Anyway, even if you don't remember him, y' might still remember me. 'Specially if you're a football fan, and you're from Sunderland.

{beat}

Or Norwich.

{beat}

PC David Edward Corner. Born – Sunderland, May the 15th, 1966. A couple of months before England won the World Cup.

So when I was still in me pram they were playing some of the games at Roker Park – y'know, Sunderland's old ground – about a mile from me mam an' dad's.

There was Chile. There was Italy. There was Russia – and their goalie, the great Lev Yashin. Y' never know, he might have walked past our house!

Amazing that. The World Cup – in Sunderland. Maybe that's why I wanted to be a footballer...?

Anyway - born Sunderland, May the 15th, 1966.

Died – Wembley Stadium, March the 24th, 1985.

{laughs} Not really. Cos I'm here, aren't I? It's just...well...plenty people wanted uz dead.

Thousands. Hundreds of thousands. Maybe millions!

Except if you were from Norwich, obviously.

{beat}

Or Newcastle…

{beat}

Mind, I could have come back from the dead - like Dixon of Dock Green. He got shot, y'know? It was a film before it went on the box. "The Blue Lamp". 1950. Jack Warner playing Dixon – which is how he got the part when it went on the telly.

In the film, he's shot by a young Dirk Bogarde. Died in hospital...came back to life on tv, five years later. And he lived on, as PC Dixon, for another 432 episodes! 'Til it got a bit far-fetched. Why, he was 80 when they made the last one! Ha'way! Would've liked to have seen him chasing a hoodie up the High Street. Trying to settle a domestic in Dawdon. Wouldn't have lasted two minutes!

Mind you, coming back from the dead? Be handy, that, if he'd been a copper these days.

Never thought I'd be a copper. Never thought I'd find a job where I was hated even more than when I was a footballer!

Course, I never knew it was going to turn out like that. Well, y' don't, do y'? Not when they're asking for your autograph, and your picture's in the paper, and the lasses are hanging 'round the door at the club, and the crowd's chanting your name.

"Living the Dream." That's what they say, isn't it? When you do something *loads* of other kids would *love* to do, if they'd been given half a chance – had half the breaks, half the talent...half the luck. I had all o' that.

Didn't know it at the time, mind. Just the way it happened. Good at footy - school team, town team, county team – the lot.... all the way to the Milk Cup final at Wembley.

Living the dream....living the nightmare.

{beat}

Me mam set the video, so I could watch meself when we got back from London. Know how many times I've watched it? Correct – never. Not once.

Well, you wouldn't, would y'?

Worst day of your life.

Worst *moment* of your life.

Live on the telly, in the days when there was hardly ANY footy on the box – apart from Match o' the Day. Only four channels back then, so if you were a footy fan, you'd be sat there with your lager and your crisps and your feet up on the settee. Audience of...I dunno how many millions. Five? 10? 20?

Doesn't matter, really. There was enough.

When videos went out of fashion, I thought that might be it, y'know? You could still read about it in books and in the papers, but you'd never actually *see* it again – unless they put it on some footy programme. Y' know: "great cock-ups of the 1980s." "Let's have a laugh at what Davey did..."

All them old videos, eh? Packed away in boxes, stuffed up in the attic. Even the charity shops won't take them now!

And then came bloody You Tube. Mind, it's not the first thing you'll find if you type in "David Corner". Nah.

You get David Beckham - *scoring* straight from a *corner*.

Aye, that's him. "Golden Balls."

Y' know what they called me on telly?

"Copper Top!" Nah – seriously!

It's Wembley, and I'm standing with the lads, right near the end of the line, just before kick-off, waiting to shake hands with some posh bloke who's going to present the Cup at the end. And all you want to do is run away as fast as y' can and get on with the game, cos it's a Cup final, and you can feel y' backside starting to go.

Anyway, he comes to me, and the camera's on uz, and Barry Davies - doing the commentary on the BBC – he says: "There's David Corner - Copper Top."

That's racist, that! "Ginger-ist." I could nick him for it, these days!

Aye – Barry Davies....baldy bastard! Mind, he didn't give uz any stick for the goal. In fact, it was like he never saw what happened.

I did though. Still do. I see it every night...when I go to bed...when I shut me eyes.

{beat}

If you watch it again, the camera goes straight to me. *He* knew who cocked it up - the TV director. Cheers mate!

You can see Benno – Gary Bennett, playing alongside uz at the back – he's waving his arm at uz. Telling uz I should have stuck the ball in row Z. "They can't score if it's up there in the crowd!" Which I'd pretty much worked out for meself, like!

Barry Davies doesn't pick up on it, though. On the telly, he just mentions the deflection.

"Own goal by Chisholm," he says.

These days they would've been showing it from a hundred different angles, wouldn't they? Analysing it, back in the studio. *They'd* know whose fault it was. Alan Shearer – aye, he would have *loved* it! Sunderland gettin' beat in a Cup final.

{Geordie accent}

"What the young lad's did there, he's give it away when, for me, he's got to purriz foot through it. Shame that, though, Sun'lun losing..."

Aye – I can just see his face. And there's another baldy! But y' can't tell, cos he's got this sun tan that never goes away! Spends all his time on the golf course, that's why.

Canny life, that. So was mine...'til I went to Wembley.

{beat}

The lads were all right about it. Didn't even get mentioned in the dressing room, after. Well, we'd lost the Cup final. Everyone was too sick to talk, really.

Drove back in the team bus the next day, and as we got near home there were fans on the side of the road and on the bridges – shouting, waving their scarves, an' that. Wasn't quite the same as 1973, when they won the FA Cup and there was about a quarter of a million there - but there were still plenty about. It was fantastic.

We'd done well to get there, to be honest, y' know? We'd been crap in the League, but – for some reason – we'd gone on this run in the Milk Cup, and you just went out there thinking you were going to win.

First couple of rounds, it's just another game. Sudden death, like, so it's not the same as the League. But you get through a couple, and suddenly you think: "Hey, we might do something here!"

Then you start talking in the dressing room, after training, and you find a few of the lads are thinking the same. Then you start winning games you shouldn't really be winning.

Like Tottenham away, when Chris saved a penalty – and Chizzy scored in the *right* end!

He did the same at Watford, in the quarter-finals. Clive Walker takes a shot, Chizzy turns his back – hits him - sends the keeper the wrong way!

And the semi-final against Chelsea - we got *two* penalties in the first leg. Westy – Colin West, big lad up front – even missed one of them, but it comes back off the keeper and he hacks in the rebound off his shin! *Horrible* goal, but you take them all day!

Chelsea fans went crackers that night. They were up in the old Main Stand. Lost, two-nowt. Probably thought: "That's us knackered. Not going to Wembley now."

And it was a big thing, that. No play-offs or Cup semi-finals there in them days. You had to get to a final to play at Wembley – or play for England. It was a massive day out: for the club, the players, the fans – everyone. And they couldn't handle it – the Chelsea lot. The fact they weren't gonna get there. Beaten by these "bladdy Norveners!"

They started kicking the old wooden seats to bits. Chucking them down on the coppers and the fans in the paddock.

There was hell on.

Should have known what to expect, really, when we went down there for the second leg.

This was the old Stamford Bridge, remember? Terraces. The Shed – where all the Chelsea nutters went. Only this time they thought they'd come on the pitch.

We'd just gone 2-1 up – 4-1 on aggregate. No way they were coming back from that. And then it all kicked off.

They were smashing up the seats...ripping chunks of concrete out o' the steps...chucking anything they could get their hands on.

I wasn't playing – I was in the stands. Big Cockney guy looks over, says: "You from San-lan?" Just shook me head! Didn't say nowt – not with *my* accent! Wasn't daft.

When we scored the third, there was a police horse on the pitch, chasing this kid through the penalty area. *Really!*

Absolute madness. We were lucky to get out alive. We had about three and a half thousand fans there, and on the way back a few of the buses had their windows put in. Young kids, most of them, doing it. Cos when you've got a convoy, the coaches don't move very fast. It's like a sitting target.

Me mate was on one of them. Brick came straight through the window – just missed the driver. Said the lad in the seat in front of him got an eyeful of glass. Blood everywhere.

Stupid, man. But that's what it was like in them days.

All-seater grounds have made a massive difference – 'specially for us coppers. CCTV everywhere. If you're sitting down, it's easier to spot the daft lads. And it's not so easy for *them* to start a chant, y'know? Bit self-conscious when there's a bloke and his lass sitting next to you with the bairns, and you're 40-odd year-old, and you're singing "We hate the Cockneys!"

In a mob, it's different.

Maybe that's why the atmosphere's not there any more?

Strange thing is, a lot of kids DO stand at matches these days, trying to get the singing going. An' they've paid top dollar for a seat! And the clubs send the stewards piling in to try to get them to sit down – even though they want them to make a noise and get the team going!

Doesn't make sense, man.

Anyway, it's great when the fans are *with* you. And the day after the final we get back to the ground, and there's – I don't know – 500, a thousand of them waiting outside? 'Cos it was a big thing. Only the third time Sunderland had been to Wembley.

First time we'd lost, mind.

So the barriers are out, to hold back the crowds, but they're all hanging over them, wanting to shake your hand. And Lenny - Lenny Ashurst - the boss, he says: "Make sure you say something to them, cos they're what the club's all about. They'll be pleased to see you!"

Aye, right.

So I gets off the bus, signs a few autographs, couple of photo's, and I gets about 10 yards down the line, and this big bloke leans over, grabs uz by the collar, drags uz over the barrier and screams in me face: "You, y'bastard! Y' lost us the bloody cup final!"

{beat}

Charming!

{beat}

Anyway, Lenny and a couple of the lads dive in, drag uz away, shove uz through the door into the ground. And that's when it all began.

The first time I realised me life might be a *bit* different from now on…

{beat}

And you know how often I'm reminded of it?

Every day.

Every.

Sodding.

Day.

It's like a life sentence – with no time off for good behaviour! No remission. No parole. "You've just got to live with it, son."

It's an open prison, mind, so I can come and go when I want. Just means I can bump into more people who can give uz dog's abuse!

You'd think, after all these years, folk might have got over it by now, y'know – it's been a canny while!

But that's football for you. It's *part* of you. It's in the blood. At least, it is, up here. And what I did's been passed on from father to son. Only, the story gets a bit mixed up – like it does, y' know? Chinese whispers.

So years later, when I was picking me kids up from school, it was: "Dad, is *that* him – the one who scored the own goal in the Cup final?" Nah - that was Chizzy.

Or it was: "Dad, is that the one who missed the penalty at Wembley?" No – that was Clive Walker!

Aye, we missed a penalty as well! Second half. Hit the post. First person to miss a penalty in a cup final at Wembley. So it wasn't just *my* fault we lost! It's just – being a local lad, maybes being ginger – nobody forgets I did *something* I shouldn't have!

103

But who remembers I cleared one off the line? Aye – saved us going a goal down in the first-half. Chris Turner comes out to block a shot, I run behind him, the ball breaks to John Deehan, the keeper's nowhere - and I'm there to block it, in the six-yard box. And does anyone ever mention *that*?

The ref had a word, mind. Said something to uz afterwards about being "sorry" – which was good of him. Neil Midgley. Died a few year back. Cancer. Only 58.

Dunno what he was sorry for…wasn't his fault.

{beat}

I just felt sorry for me mam and dad. They got it everywhere they went. Got so bad, sometimes they didn't want to leave the house.

We lived near the ground, so I used to walk to training every day, with me boots under me arm. Do y' think Ronaldo does that? Or Lionel Messi? *{ironic laugh}*

I could hear it the street, when people went past. When I went for me paper. At the garage…but mostly in the pub. It was like they took it *personally*. Like I'd done it on purpose, just to spite them, y' know?

Had plenty of fights over it.

Maybes I should've just stayed at home and let it blow over – but spend the rest of me life in front of the telly!

Nah. Didn't fancy that.

So I went out. Had a few beers. Had a laugh…which some folk didn't like.

"What's he laughing at? Useless ginger get. Lost us the bloody Cup final".

That's usually how it started.

One of them ended up in Durham Crown Court. Amateur boxer. GBH. Left uz with a fractured eye socket, broken jaw, stitches in me lip. I've got a metal plate in me head to remind uz.

He got off, an' all. Said it was self-defence!

I must have been hitting his fist too hard with me face…

That one got in the papers, but most times, I just didn't bother. I wasn't in the force then, and it was too much hassle to go to the coppers. Plus, it would only give some other nutter the idea of having a go.

Once, in The Londonderry – old pub in the town centre …I'm standing there with a few mates – who were great, by the way. They looked after uz. Tried to watch me back.

But this one time, I'm standing there, minding me own business, and this lad says: "Davey?" And I turns round, thinking he wants to talk football. And he just smacks uz right on the side of the jaw - smashes me teeth in - then legs it out the door.

I mean, what can y do?

It's just not *normal*, is it? To hold a grudge for all these years?

I mean, ha'way – how many games have we played since then?

Someone must have done *something* worse than me in all that time, surely!?

'Spose you've got to be philosophical about these things.

And who was the greatest football philosopher? Bill Shankly? *{mock Scottish accent}* "Football's not a matter of life and death – it's more serious than that!"

Only, *he* wasn't being serious when he said it. It's a good one, though.

What about Eric Cantona, when he jumped into the crowd and kung fu-kicked that kid who'd been giving him some stick, after he got sent off at Crystal Palace?

I know how he felt!

He got a nine-month ban, 20 thousand quid fine, two weeks in prison knocked down to 120 hours community service. Would've been worth it, though. I'd have settled for that.

And you know what – after he came back, the next season they made him Footballer of the Year! Really. Who says crime doesn't pay…?

Mind, it was the Press who voted for him. And that was only cos he filled their papers every day.

Remember what he said, when he had that Press conference after he'd been banned? *{mock-French accent}*

"When ze seagulls follow ze trawler, it's because zey think sardines will be thrown into ze sea."

{beat}

What a load o' bollocks!

Aye - and that's what *he* said about it, afterwards! When he went back to Man United. Steve Bruce told uz this one: Eric's in the dressing room, back in training, first time after the ban. And Brucey says to him: "So, Eric, what was all that about? Y' know, the seagulls an' that?"

And Cantona says: "Yeah, it was a load of shit – but it sounded pretty good, no?"

Seriously – even he didn't have a clue what he was on about!

{beat}

Nah – the greatest football philosopher was a bloke called Albert Camus.

Ever heard of him?

Another French gadgie. Well, French-Algerian. Played in goal for Racing University of Algeria, 'til he got polio. Had to give up. Went on to write books an' stuff. Won the Nobel Prize for Literature, 1957. Canny, that. Not even Beckham's got one o' them! Which is no surprise, by the way…

Camus' mate said to him once: "Which do you prefer – football or theatre?" Know what he said? "Football – without hesitation!"

It *was* like a theatre, though – walking out at Wembley. Just so much noise. From *everywhere*. Rolling down off the terraces…crashing round your ears. Deafening…

But I wasn't that nervous.

You would've thought, at 18, wouldn't you? But I was looking around, thinking: "What's all the noise about? Who are they cheering for? It can't be us. It can't be for me…." But it was. It was just…incredible.

I mean, the new Wembley's good, y' know – don't get uz wrong. Eighty thousand seats, not a bad view in the house. No pillars, no girders, no-one shoving you or pushing and pulling you from behind, trying to get past so they can see, or pissing in y' pocket cos they're all squashed up and they've had a few beers and they can't get to the bogs in time!

No, really – I've seen it!

Nah, it's not like the old days. Not like the old Wembley.

There was a hundred thousand there, and they said about 70,000 of them were from Sunderland.

107

Well, not just Sunderland. I mean, from everywhere roundabouts. From Murton, from Blackhall – all the Durham pit villages. From Ashington, from Bedlington – cos when the miners went up into the Northumberland coalfields – all them years ago, when there *was* coal - they never forgot their roots.

Aye - the Shields lot, the Jarrow and the Hebburn lads, Billingham, Hartlepool. And the London branch, of course. Second-biggest supporters' club in London, behind Man United. And that's only cos all the Man U fans were born there!

Not like our lot. Follow the team for love, not the glory. Just as well, mind. Nowt much glorious since '73…

It's that connection, y'know? With home. Even though you can be a million miles away.

Maybe lots of places pull you back like that? I dunno.

Sunderland does, though.

The whole North East does, to be fair. It's in your blood. Y' DNA. Was for me. That's why it took uz years to leave.

{beat}

Always wanted to be a footballer.

Only ever wanted to play for Sunderland.

Went to Oldham first, though. 17 year-old. Lasted three weeks. They put uz in digs, and I told the landlady I was poorly.

I was - I was homesick. Jumped on a train - never went back.

Then Everton took uz on. Only lasted a *week* there! Good move, that, wasn't it, jacking it in there? The year we lost at Wembley...the year I did what I did...they won the League *and* the European Cup Winners' Cup! Gary Lineker, Peter Reid, big Neville Southall – all o' them......

Could've been me....

{beat}

Anyway. Albert Camus – back to him.

His most famous quote, he said *{mock French accent}*: "Whatever I know about life, I learned from football."

Sounds good that – if he wants to know about being kicked up a height, left out of the team when you think you're the dog's bollocks, or being screamed at and spat at and having your lights punched out cos y' didn't stick the ball in the stands cos you lost us the bloody cup final!

{beat}

Actually, what he said was: "After many years, during which I saw many things, what I know most surely about morality and the duty of man, I owe to sport."

Basically, he was talking about fair play. About having a bit of bottle. Sticking up for your mates.

Team work: You don't get very far in football if you haven't got it. And we didn't have much of it at Sunderland, after the Cup final.

Got relegated that season.

After Wembley we played 12 more games. Only won one o' them.

Last match of the season, at Roker Park - y' know what the crowd was? Nine thousand. *Nine* thousand.

There'd been *seventy* thousand of them at Wembley.

They'd gone all that way - to the other end of the country – to watch us lose. Two months later, they couldn't even be bothered to leave the house and walk round the block to see us.

That's football fans for you… Lenny got sacked soon after.

And then they brought in Lawrie McMenemy. Or, as he became known, Lawrie Mackem-enemy!

Highest paid manager in English football, he was. And the highest-paid flop.

Mind, he was good for me.

You only like a manager if he plays you – so I hated just about all o' mine! But Lawrie gave uz me longest run in the team. And *he* ended up being screamed at by the fans even more than me. So that was good. Took the heat off uz for a bit!

When he arrived he said he'd take us out of the Second Division. And he did...took us into the Third!

It was like he was on a kamikaze mission, to ruin *us* and ruin himself at the same time.

Virtually got run out of town in the end.

And what happened? He finished up in the Football Managers' Hall of Fame!

Seriously. Some managers have made a canny living out of being sacked and walking off with a few years' salary. It's the only job where you make a fortune out of being crap.

The best story about Lawrie – well, there's a few of them tell it, but I was there. In fact, I was right in the middle of it. No, the one that shows you how bad we were...

We were training at Roker Park. On the pitch, day before a game – true this. Right at the end of the session, Lawrie has us lining up in formation and kicking off.

We're not playing anyone, mind.

No opposition.

Sounds daft, but it's just so's we can, like, go through the motions. Rehearse your moves, y'know? So's you know what to do when it's for real.

So we kick-off, and Eric Gates passes to Davey Swindlehurst.

He knocks it wide to Jack Lemon – Paul's his real name, but he gets Jack.

He knocks it to George Burley, and Lawrie shouts: "Back to the keeper and we'll start again."

So George gives it to me, and I turn to pass back to Hezzy – Iain Hesford - who's our goalie. Only it bobbles, just as I'm playing it, and it loops up off me shin.

And Hezzy's out of his goal, and he has to hurl himself backwards, and he *just* manages to tip it over the bar! Hell of a save!

And the lads are *pissing* themselves - but Lawrie's going c*rackers*!

He's shouting: "Bloody hell – there's only *you lot* out there, and we're nearly gettin' beat!"

Still makes uz laugh, that one! Don't think Lawrie would laugh about it, even now!

And poor Hezzy's dead. Aye – a few years ago. 54. Heart attack. He was a big lad, mind. Vicar at his funeral said he was: "larger than life." See the size of him? Larger than most lads I knew.

Vicar told this story of when Hezzy's playing for Blackpool: They're losing, and Hezzy's having a nightmare, and some kid behind the goal chucks a pie at him. So he walks round the back of the net, picks it up and scoffs it! Honest! Which probably didn't help, like, when he was carrying a few extra pounds…

Surprised Lawrie never had a heart attack when he was with us. He said going to Sunderland was "the biggest regret" of his career. Don't worry, fella – all the fans feel the same!

It was funny, 'cos he was from the North East, but he'd made his name down the other end of the country, at Southampton. Whenever he came back, it was like a big deal, y' know - they loved him. "The Genial Geordie" – that's what the papers called him. He thought he just had to turn up, and everything would fall into place.

So he comes here, loses his first five games, we don't even score a goal – and it's downhill from then on, 'til he packs his bags, clears his house and flies off to Florida – aye, that's what he did. Sold his story to The Sun, so it was all over the back page the next day. By which time he was lying on a beach! Even the club didn't know 'til they read about it.

That was *his* way out of a bad decision: Jump on a plane and disappear.

Wish I could've done summat like that.

{beat}

Every day y' make decisions, don't you? When am I getting out o' bed? What'll I have for me breakfast? Do I need me coat?

Most o' them you do without thinking.

Just as well, really, else you'd never get anything done.

Some of them – the bigger ones – you need to weigh up: If I do that, this'll happen. So maybe I won't do it. I'll do summat else.

When I was a lad, they had these things on the telly.

Public Information films, they called them. Common sense, really. Don't have them now, cos folk don't like to be told. 'Specially not the kids.

Trouble is, *they* do a lot of things without thinking – and more often than not it's us coppers who have to clear up the mess.

Anyway – they were canny films.

"Don't be an Amber Gambler." Remember that one? Don't jump the lights, in case you meet someone who's jumping them from the other direction.

Sound, that. I've had to scrape a few boy racers out their cars.

Not nice.

{posh voice} "Polish a floor and put a rug on it – you might as well set a mantrap!" What about that one?

Or that bloke – Joe - with a hanky on his head and his missus – Petunia – and the "sailin' dingey!"

They were good though: Don't swim in deep water. Don't go off with strangers.

Little bits of advice, just meant to stick in your mind. Help you make the right decisions. Most of them were everyday things, but some could change your life.

Like mine did.

{beat}

What you hear most, from football coaches, if the ball's in that sort of position, running away from goal, down towards the corner flag, they'll say: "hump it over the dead-ball line, far as y' can."

"If in doubt, put it out. They can't score if it's in row Z."

Football's own little Public Information films. Maybes I just wasn't listening?

{beat}

I'd not been well, leading up to the Cup final. I had this disease. Can't remember what they call it, but me gums were growing over me teeth! I know - sounds horrible. Looked pretty horrible, an' it felt pretty horrible. I couldn't eat properly. In four weeks I lost about a stone.

I came back to work – to training – the day they were taking the photos for the Cup final programme. And I thought I looked tidy, y'know? Quite trim.

You look at the pictures now, I look gaunt. Drained. I said to Frank, the trainer: "Frank - how d'y' think I'm looking?"

I thought he'd say I looked good, y'know, cos I'd lost a few pound. But I'll never forget it.

He said: "Son – you look *pathetic*."

And y' know what? Of all the things people said to uz about the Cup final, that was one of the nicest!

I should've known, really. To be a centre-half, you've got to be good in the air – obviously. Y'know, jump up and head the ball away - maybes have a bit of pace, be able to sprint when you have to. Bit o' nous, so you can read the game – know what the guy you're marking's going to do if he gets the ball – if you let him get the ball.

'Cos you've got to be a bit of a nasty bastard, an'all. Do just about anything to stop him putting that ball in the net.

I don't mean sticking the boot in….well, not every time!

Just not letting yourself be bullied, y'know? They call it "getting your retaliation in first." Sounds better like that. It's just letting the striker know you're there.

But you also need a bit o' beef – and I'd lost that in the weeks before the final, when I was ill.

What you do, when the ball's going out, like it was then - you try to shield it. You stick out your backside, and use that as, like, a buffer. "There you are mate, try 'n get round that!"

By the time they have, the ball'll be over the line, out of play, the ref's given a goal-kick, the keeper boots it upfield and you start all over again.

That's how it should have been.

You've seen it a thousand times before. I'd done it a thousand times before.

And I know what y' thinking: "Cup final...hundred thousand there...young lad...18...tryin' to be a smart arse..."

But it wasn't like that!

It was instinct...and I got it wrong. I just…got it wrong....

{beat}

Philosophy again. Football's all about kidology.

Nah, you can't get a degree in it. Mind, these days...!

Anyway, it's all about kidding yourself you're better than them. Especially when you're not. It's the same in *every* dressing room, up and down the country, right across the world. From the dads with their bairns in the park on a Saturday morning, to Cup finals like ours.

Same old story, week after week...and we fall for it, every time.

"Come on, y' can beat this lot – they're crap! Have y' seen the size of that skinny lad, the full-back? A breath o' wind an' he'll be on his backside.

"And look at the keeper! Couldn't catch a cold.

"That lad, the midfielder everyone goes on about. I've seen him. Couldn't pass water.

"On our day, we can beat anyone," which is true mind! About the only thing that is.

"So let's get straight in from the off. Keep it tight. Keep it simple. And don't forget – nowt daft!"

{beat}

That was the bit I forgot.

{beat}

We'd actually beaten Norwich at their place in the League, 3-1 - the week before the final. Important, as well, cos we were both near the bottom of the League.

I played in that one, so I had a canny idea I'd be playing at Wembley. Me mam and dad couldn't be sure, mind. But they were fans, so they would've been going anyway.

They didn't drive, so they went down, early morning - supporters' bus. Me? Only found out for sure on the day of the match.

I was sharing a room with Jack Lemon. Nah, I've told y', not that one! He was a film star.

If you don't remember "Dixon o' Dock Green" you won't remember Jack Lemmon. "Some Like it Hot"? Him and Walter Matthau – "The Odd Couple"? No? Never mind.

Anyway, Lenny comes up to the room and says to Jack: "Sorry, son." And he's gutted, but deep down he knew he wasn't gonna get picked.

But then Lenny turns to me and says: "Davey, you're in."

And I'm flying.

Thing was, I couldn't tell me mam and dad! No mobile phones in them days. No laptops, i-pads – nowt like that.

If you didn't have a phone in the house, you had to nip out to the nearest call box with a fistful of change. Tell that to the kids today, they'll think you're off another planet!

So me folks didn't actually know I was playing 'til they got to Wembley and heard me name being read out over the tannoy!

Amazing, that, when you think of it. And even now, after all the stick over all the years, they've never wished I hadn't been playing. I mean – your son, at 18, in a Cup final.

In fact, I was the youngest player ever to play for Sunderland in a Cup final at Wembley. Still am.

Not many folk remember that, do they? I do, though. Proud o' that.

{beat}

I had a canny enough career when I did leave Sunderland.

Went to Orient for a while. Player of the Year at Darlington. Helped get them back into the League after they'd dropped out, then got them promoted to the Third Division.

Played for England in the under-20s World Cup in Russia. Kept some kid called Tony Adams out of the team – wonder what happened to him…?

The day I came back from Russia, they had a big party for uz round me mam and dad's. All the family there – homecoming hero, y'know?

And just as I stepped through the door, the telly's on, and it's "Football Focus".

And I swear, I haven't even said "hiya" when the bloke on the box says: "And England went out of the under-20 World Cup in Russia

117

when they lost, thanks to an own goal by Sunderland's David Corner."

And the atmosphere - it's like a balloon that someone's just stuck a pin in, and it's gone - bang! Let's just say I've been to better parties....

Finished up playing at Gateshead, 'til me knees gave out. Did me cruciate ligament. They could probably fix it now – but not then.

Didn't really know what I'd do, after that: Ex-footballer. Dodgy knees. Used to taking plenty of stick. Hadn't really thought I'd be in me 30s an' looking for work.

Then I'm on a stag do with some mates, and one of them's a copper. And he says:

"Why don't you join the force?"

And I says: "Me, a copper?!"

The number of fights I'd had, I didn't think they'd want uz – or let uz in! But I got an interview for Durham Police. They said: "What about this incident in 1991 – arrested for being drunk and disorderly?"

I said: "It was a learning curve."

That's what they always say in football, isn't it, when they lose? "We'll learn from it."

And I got away with it! So there I am - first day out on patrol on me own – 'bout 18 months into the job. Still a bit green. And I'm in Seaham.

And there's a call to say there's been reports of a fight on The Avenue – big street, running right through the town.

So the blue light's on, and I'm straight there.

Thing is, I know I have to be quick, 'cos all coppers love a scrap. Any second, there'll be 40-odd pandas charging to the same door to get a bit o' the action.

Anyway, I'm first on the scene.

And when I get there, there's this big bloke standing outside in the street – shirt off...blood all over.

And he's saying: "I've killed him...I've killed him..."

He kicked off a bit, like, when he saw me – but I got the cuffs on an' had him nicked before the back-up team got there.

And I'd never seen a real live – well, real *dead* - body before, so I was a bit nosey, y'know? Wanted to see what he'd done to the other bloke.

So I says to the other guys: "Keep an eye on him, will y'? I'm going inside."

And I goes in, and the paramedics are there. Only no-one dares make a move – cos this bloke's not dead...yet. He's standing there in the middle of the room, absolutely *covered* in blood.

I mean, he's just *claret* - head to toe. He's changed colour.

And there's this gash across his forehead, an' it's so deep you can almost see his brains...Turned me stomach.

But he's just standing there, taking nee notice of anyone. Like he's in a trance.

And they're trying to talk to him, but he's just staring straight ahead. And no-one dares do owt, cos y' don't know what this fella's gonna do next.

So I goes in, and his eyes just lock straight on to mine. And it's weird. His head follows uz round the room, and he's just, like, staring at uz.

119

And then, suddenly, slowly, he says: "Davey?"

And I says: "All right mate?" He *wasn't*, like! *{laughs}*

And he's still looking straight at uz, and he says: "Davey Corner?"

And I says: "Aye, that's me, mate."

And he says: "Davey man........why didn't y' kick it out?"
{laughs}

Y'know, he's *dying*, and all he can think about is the bloody Cup final!

And this, by now, it's like *twelve years* after!

And I says to him: "I dunno mate – but I do know you should go to hospital."

And he says: "Do y' think so, Davey?"

And I says: "Aye."

And he says: "Well if you think so, Davey, that's what I'll do..."

And he lets the paramedics lead him out through the door – blood dripping everywhere – and he climbs into the ambulance, and he's carted off to hospital.

And the sergeant sees him going, and he says: "Well done, Davey – fine bit of policing, that!"

Course, he didn't know the full story...and I wasn't gonna tell him!

So that day I *was* a hero – cos I helped save a guy's life.

{beat}

Football, y'know – you lose a game and you hear them say: "*tragic* mistake, there, that led to the goal..." But it's not, man. It's never that bad.

It was me life...but it *is* only a game. What happened to me wasn't a tragedy.

{beat}

Before the Cup final, everyone's thinking: "Great – beat this lot, and we'll qualify for Europe next season." Which would have been a big thing, cos they'd only been there once, after they won the FA Cup in '73.

I knew lads who'd been too young then, to go away and watch the team playing abroad.

They'd waited all that time. 12 years! Seems like nothing, now.

But they said, if we won – passports ready - they'd go to the first game, wherever it was: Russia, Albania, back o' beyond - didn't matter.

Thing is, even if we *had* won, we wouldn't have played in Europe. No English team did, for the next five years. Six for Liverpool. They all got banned.

Because two months after Wembley, and what I did, there was the Heysel Disaster.

Strange, isn't it? People remember Bradford – the fire, an' that.

An' Hillsborough, o' course. Couldn't forget that.

But Heysel's a bit of blur. Maybe cos it happened abroad?

Belgium, if you'd forgotten. Brussels. European Cup final - Liverpool and Juventus.

Fans had been drinking all day – which was new to most of them. I mean, y' couldn't do that at home. Not then.

1985: Pubs opened for lunch. Shut again about two. Back open, half six. Most places, the shutters came down again, half 10.

Twenty-five past 10, you'd get a stampede to the bar for last orders! Crazy.

So lots of these Liverpool lads are well tanked-up by the time they get to the ground, cos it's like being on holiday.

And you'd think, cos it's Brussels – the capital – and cos it's a big Cup final, you'd think it would be a canny stadium. Y'know, up-to-date. New seats. Fresh lick o' paint. Make it smart, like.

You look at the pictures, now – and it was an absolute *dump*. Even the Head of Belgian Police called it: "a death trap." Afterwards, mind. Bit late, then…

The terraces were falling apart. Bits of concrete everywhere. Old-fashioned turnstiles....and old-fashioned coppers – they didn't know what to expect. Didn't know what hit them.

In them days, football fans were just like cattle. You herded them in, whacked them around with sticks to keep them in line.

Squeeze them all through the gates, then you keep them in their pens. But if you *treat* people like animals - it's no wonder they *behave* like animals.

An' they follow the leader. So when the trouble breaks out – and no-one really knows who started it – they all just pile in.

There's a line of Belgian police, and a chicken wire fence, stuck up between the Liverpool lot and what's supposed to be a neutral area – only it's full of Italians. Not the hard lads, mind. They were at the other end. So this lot weren't exactly up for a scrap.

There's a hole in the wire, and the Liverpool fans start making it bigger – and then they're coming through. There were plenty of coppers there – but most of them were *outside* the ground, and the ones inside couldn't get in touch cos their walkie-talkies were on the blink!

So there's pandemonium, and everyone in this neutral bit legs it to the far end to get away from the fightin'. An' there's this wall. An' they climb on it, and think about jumping – but there's a massive drop on the other side, so they're trapped.

And by now it's a stampede. And this is a *real* one. They're not looking for the bar, for last orders. They're scrambling for their lives.

Some of them got away. But then the wall collapsed. And the people spilled out.

Bloke who was there said it was like sand, the way they all just poured out through the cracks. Like an egg-timer, y'know? Only it was bodies...

And when you're in that situation, you'll do anything to get out. So folk were climbing over the ones on the bottom of the pile. Standing on them. *Real people*, gasping for breath under their feet. But you couldn't stop to help cos you'd be swept under as well.

Just...horrific.

[beat]

And they still played the game. I remember sitting at home, watching it on telly, and they're tellin' you kick off's been put back "cos of the trouble." And they're saying people have been hurt, but they're not saying folk have actually *died*.

And they waited two hours, and they played the game – 'cos they thought there'd be more bother if they didn't. And all the while, outside in the car park, the bodies were lying there, waiting to be carted off.

Unbelievable... Did it matter who won? Not really.

One-nil, Juventus, if you're interested.

There *were* numbers that shouldn't be forgotten, though: 350. That's how many were injured.

And 39. That's how many died.

At first they said: "39 Juventus fans...39 Italians." But it wasn't.

It was actually 32 Italians, four Belgians, two French fellas and a guy from Northern Ireland. Aye – Northern Ireland.

Called him Patrick Radcliffe. Ever heard of him? Thought not. But he's there, on the list of the dead. In amongst all them Giovannis and Lucianos and Luigis. There was even a Barbara.

Bright lad, Patrick. Went to Oxford University. Worked for the EEC – as it was then: The European Economic Community. Archives department.

From East Belfast. Grew up there in the '60s and '70s, so he'd probably seen his share of bad stuff and thought he'd escaped from all that crap: The bombings, the shootings, the stupid waste of life.

Been living in Brussels with his missus for five years, and you know what? He wasn't even a football fan.

Had a mate – a Dutch lad – who was dead keen. Ticket going spare, so he tagged along for the night. Just for the company and the craic. Never went home. He was 37.

Right place, wrong choice. Now *that's* a real tragedy.

Mine wasn't.

{beat}

And what was it? My "Crime of the Century?"

{deep sigh}

All right...so it's a minute into the second half.

Nil-nil. Everything to play for.

Long ball down our right – their left.

It was going out. I could have wellied it back down the line, 'cos I had plenty of time. But I thought I'd just shield it, y'know, like they do...let it run out...take the goal kick. We'd turn round, jog back upfield, Chris – the goalie - would lump it up to halfway and we'd start all over again.

{beat}

Glanced over me shoulder and saw their lad - John Deehan - coming towards uz.

"Dixie" they called him. "Dixie" Deehan? Like "Dixie Dean"? Might have to explain that to the young 'uns...

Y'know what I got after the final? "Foxy"...as in "what the Foxy Deehan?!" Think about it...

Anyway, Dixie Deehan's coming up behind uz, so I thought I'd try a dummy. Y'know - dip me shoulder one way, so he'd go the other. Only needed half a second and we'd be safe. Only, he came round on me blind side.

Clever shite.

Pushed the ball through me legs – aye, a "nutmeg", just to really take the piss!

Then he sprints into the box, and I can't catch him. He pulls the ball back. Chizzy gets a foot in – Gordon Chisholm – but it drops straight to this guy called Asa Hartford.

Right foot shot, 12 yards out. It's not that hard. And it's going straight to Chrissy Turner – easy save. No problem.

Only Chiz gets in the way.

He's trying to block it, but it slides off his chest, and it goes straight in the bottom corner. Keeper - no chance. 1-0 Norwich.

Turns out it's the only goal of the game. All down to me.

And that's it – my life, changed forever. Never be the same again.

"Lost us the bloody cup final!"

Simple as that.

{beat}

And what would I do now? If I was back near the corner flag...ball rolling out...Dixie bloody Deehan sneaking up behind uz?

All them fans.

Chance to win the Cup.

Chance to be a hero.

Would I stick me foot through it?

Clear me lines?

Put the ball into row Z?

{beat}

Naaah!

If I'd done that...no-one would ever have heard of uz!

Anyway, I suppose you all want to see it now, yeah? It's what you've been waiting for?

{You Tube footage of the winning goal from the 1985 Milk Cup final – Davey watches it and notices something}

Yeah, that's it. Doesn't get any better...woah! Hang on.

{shouts to technician at the back of the room}

Stop it there. Rewind. Just – *rewind* it, 'til the ball's being played through. Now, stop – just as Hartford's taking his shot. Look! Deehan – John Deehan! He's…offside. He's *offside*!

So…that goal…the ref saying "sorry"…*my life*!

SHIT!!

The End